The
Burdensome

Joy

of
Preaching

The
Burdensome

Joy

of
Preaching

James Earl Massey

Abingdon Press
Nashville

The Burdensome Joy of Preaching

Copyright © 1998 by Abingdon Press

Library of Congress Cataloging-in-Publication Data

Massey, James Earl.
  The burdensome joy of preaching: reflections on the pulpit of experience/James Earl Massey.
    p.   cm.
  Includes indexes.
  ISBN 0-687-05069-3 (alk. paper)
  1. Preaching.   2. Massey, James Earl.   I. Title.
  BV4211.2   IN PROCESS
  251—dc21   98-18599
                                                                        CIP

98 99 00 01 02 03 04 05 06 07 — 10 9 8 7 6 5 4 3 2 1

MANUFACTURED IN THE UNITED STATES OF AMERICA

To the friends and sharers
I have known and served as
preacher in the following settings:

Metropolitan Church, Detroit, Michigan
(Senior Pastor, 1954–76 Pastor-at-Large since 1976)

Anderson University, Anderson, Indiana
(Campus Minister, 1969–77)

"Christian Brotherhood Hour" radio broadcast
(Speaker, 1977–82)

Tuskegee University, Tuskegee, Alabama
(Dean of the Chapel, 1984–90)

Park Place Church of God, Anderson, Indiana
(Preacher-in-Residence, 1994–95)

CONTENTS

PREFACE

This book is an expanded treatment of the William E. Conger Lectures on Biblical Preaching, given in 1995 at Beeson Divinity School, Samford University, in Birmingham, Alabama. Dean Timothy George graciously invited me to deliver the Conger Lectures, and I am grateful to him and to Dr. C. Richard Wells for making my assignment and stay such an enriching set of experiences. It was also my delight to meet Colonel and Mrs. William Conger, who not only attended all of the lectures, but also were generously attentive to this lecturer through many other kindnesses.

The substance of this book treats the privileged task of preaching, with particular focus on pulpit work as the preacher experiences it.

The mind and mood of our times can be summed up in that inclusive word *experience,* a word that reflects our awareness of the multiple effects of life upon us and the wide range of our contacts and resultant impressions. We use the word so readily, sometimes preceded by a modifying adjective or adverb to show its many-sidedness, as when we speak about having had a good or bad experience or of some experience as a memorable, meaningful, or life-changing one. We speak about an experience as valid, valuable, hazardous, problematic, painful, or treasured.

The word *experience* fits our human condition quite well, and the many adjectives or adverbs we associate with it all testify that we have lived, perceived, and understood some personal happening in a certain way.

In this treatment of the pulpit experience, some reflections are offered about the content and context of this "happening," which involves both preacher and hearers in a deeply personal and eternally meaningful way. In the chapters offered here, attention is given first to the preacher's sense of the *inward* side of the task, and next to the *outward* side of preaching. The focus then shifts to a consideration of the desired *togetherness* that earnest preachers seek to experience with their hearers, followed by some reflections on the kind of planning necessary for the *eventfulness* that preaching was ordained by God to effect.

In preparing this book I have sifted my thoughts after almost fifty years of pulpit experiences, as well as the thoughts and experiences of many other preachers. I pray that what I have traced in writing here will stimulate, remind, inform, and encourage others who bear the necessary and perennial responsibility to prepare and to preach.

It is necessary to add that selected aspects of this theme and earlier versions of these materials were used in several other settings: in 1994 as the Ritz Lectures at Winebrenner Theological Seminary, as the Miller Chapel Lectures at Anderson School of Theology, and as the Swartley Lectures at Eastern Baptist Theological Seminary; in 1991 as the E. Stanley Jones Lectures on Preaching at Boston University School of Theology; in 1990 as the inaugural J. Myron Taylor Lectures on Preaching at the Westwood Christian Foundation, adjacent to the campus of the University of California at Los Angeles; in 1986 as the Jesse and Fannie Northcutt Lectures on Preaching at Southwestern Baptist Theological Seminary; and in 1983 as the Annual Ministry Lectures at Ashland Theological Seminary. To my hosts, friends, and colleagues in each of these theological settings, I am deeply grateful, especially for the opportunity the invitations allowed for me to meet the honorees (and family members) of several of the named lectureships. This all-too-brief acknowledgment of them is made from a deep well of rich memories and appreciation.

Last of all, it should be reported that chapter 5 is a sermon that was delivered to fellow members of the Academy of Homiletics, assembled for the closing worship service of the 1994 annual meeting, held at Duke University Divinity School. I am eternally grateful to Dr. O. C. Edwards, Academy President, and to my many esteemed teaching colleagues for the honor I experienced as their chosen preacher for that service. In keeping with the Advent season, I preached about the person and work of Jesus, the central figure of our faith. Not long afterward, while at Samford University to deliver the Conger Lectures, I used the sermon again during an all-university chapel service. Thus its inclusion here.

James Earl Massey

CHAPTER ONE

The Inward Side of Preaching

The act of preaching involves preacher and hearers in a series of dynamic moments: It is a bid, on God's initiative, for an interaction that can grant comfort or the pressure of challenge, pulling upon the inwardness of one and all. As for the preacher's experience of that inward pressure, Samuel H. Miller once referred to it as "the joy and embarrassment of preaching."[1] The inimitable Gardner C. Taylor uniquely described that sense of inward pull as "the sweet torture of Sunday morning."[2] I have long looked upon preaching, and graciously experienced it, as a burdensome joy. It is "burdensome" because of the way the preparation and delivery aspects of the pulpit task weigh upon the preacher's selfhood—and with so many unique demands. But preaching is also a "joy" because of the divine purpose that makes it necessary and the redeeming eventfulness that it can effect for those who receive it with faith and openness.

The Burden of Preaching

Those who preach know that ours is a work of mingled drama and distress. It is dramatic because it has to do with being on

---

1. Samuel H. Miller, *The Dilemma of Modern Beliefs,* The Lyman Beecher Lectures 1962 (New York: Harper and Bros., 1963), ix.
2. Gardner C. Taylor, interviewed in *Leadership* 2, 3 (Summer 1981): 16-29.

business for God, while the distress issues from that awesome feeling of being immediately responsible for, and so personally exposed in, our work. The responsibility, then, can be sensed as a burden.

Students of the Hebrew text of the Old Testament will recall Isaiah's frequent use of the word *massa* to describe what speaking for God made Isaiah feel. The term is used quite often to express some physical load under which an animal or a person labors, but Isaiah used it to reflect the weighty responsibility of his prophetic task (Isa. 13:1; 14:28; 15:1; 17:1; 19:1; 21:1, 11, 13; 22:1, 25; 23:1). Many recent Bible versions have translated the Hebrew *massa* as "oracle," departing from the King James Version's "burden"; but the notion of heaviness is still to be understood as being associated with the task of proclaiming the oracle, since the responsibility of handling it falls so weightily upon the one charged by God to voice it. Isaiah was not alone in his use of the term, as a look at Lamentations 2:14; Nahum 1:1; Zechariah 9:1; 12:1; and Malachi 1:1 will make clear. As those prophets considered the awesome service God had appointed them to render, they also described the nature of it and their experience of it as a "burden."

The preacher's sense of being burdened as God's speaking servant is compounded by the attendant awareness of being so personally exposed. One does feel exposed, for one is speaking not only *about* God but also *for* God. This task can be felt as an inward pressure—indeed, as a distress—which is why some preachers opt to use humor as they begin the sermon, or they might deal in levels of confession throughout the sermon, seeking to find some measure of relief from the pressure through the spirit of a lighter sharing. We all know that some measure of relief comes when we achieve rapport with others, when we are assured that they have to some extent identified with us, for this grants the pressured self a sense of companionship, on the one hand, and a wider working space, on the other hand.

It might seem strange that preachers feel so burdened and exposed in doing their given work, since preaching is usually done in the communal context of worship, with the companionship of fellow believers as an encouraging resource. But the fact is that no matter how many loving sharers are present and participating in worship, the one preaching to them inevitably stands at some distance from the people precisely because he or she has been sent to speak *to* them rather than *for* them. The speaking preacher is initially pressed in ways that the hearers are not pressed. Our very service keeps us open to that pressure, and that pressure is greatly intensified when our concern to share God's message seems lightly regarded or is blatantly resisted. To feel put off or rejected rather than accepted can give one a threatening sense of aloneness and a heavy feeling of dreadful exposure.

The prophet Elijah experienced this. You will recall his almost absurd cry to God as he felt pressured by the murderous tactics of an unrelenting Jezebel. He lamented, "I alone am left, and they seek to take my life" (1 Kings 19:14 NEB). The prophet Jeremiah openly confessed his felt distress to God, even daring to curse the day of his birth because his work for God was being steadily disregarded by some and openly defied by many others:

> Cursed be the day
> on which I was born.
> The day when my mother bore me,
> let it not be blessed!
> .   .   .   .
> Why did I come forth from the womb
> to see toil and sorrow,
> and spend my days in shame? (Jer. 20:14, 18)

Yes, "personal exposure" is the right expression to use to describe the preaching experience, because we who preach are always under scrutiny—and sometimes we are under the judgment of those who differ with us. It is not unusual to be met with cautious or suspicious eyes as we look out and see those who have gathered before us.

Pulpit ministry opens us to people's curiosity about public figures. More often than not, the preacher is an intense personality, and people hunger to know as much as possible about such persons. (Preachers are even curious about each other, always seeking an inside knowledge of each other, interrogating each other about reading choices, experiences, springs of thought, methods used in preparation of sermons, and more.) But all humans have an eagerness to know and understand each other as we are. Even now, some are perhaps asking inwardly what kind of person this writer is. Those who preach are like all other people in having emotional responses to life; just as we raise questions about others, so also there are those who raise questions about us. There is no way around being at the center of things when we are in public view through public service; there is no way around feeling at the edge of the crowd, even as we long to be regarded as an accepted part of that crowd.

The late Dag Hammarskjöld understood this. Like the rest of us, he struggled long and hard with the heavy weight of self-exposure. His work as Secretary-General of the United Nations was heavy, tiring, and generally discouraging. On July 6, 1961, two months before his tragic death in a plane crash in the Congo, Hammarskjöld wrote this in his diary:

> Tired
> and lonely,
> So tired
> the heart aches.
> .   .   .   .   .
> It is now,
> Now, that you must not give in.
> On the paths of the others
> Are resting places,

Places in the sun
Where they can meet.
But this
Is your path,
And it is now,
Now, that you must not fail.[3]

The Burden of Felt Limitations

The exposed inwardness we feel in the pulpit is compounded by a felt limitation in the use of words as we preach. Every earnest preacher knows the suffering that attends the attempt to make what writer Shirley Hazzard refers to as "the testimony of the accurate word."[4]

How often it is that we who preach return home sad, lamenting the distance between the vision that fired our hearts before preaching and the meager expression we gave of it in the sermon. The dream we had thrilled us, but the delivery we gave of it shamed us. It is a situation we all know too well. How difficult it is to testify with an "accurate word." We long to preach with adequacy and fullness, but the quest to do so seems unending. It is as if God has placed before us a line we cannot cross, ruling that the Word must be known and heard in the circumstances of our limitations, that not only is our agonizing with language a test to our intent, but also our very struggle is part of the process that reveals God's will to the hearers. The quest for the right word achieves its end in the miracle of hearing; we must, therefore, speak what we *must,* what we are sent to share, and the listening ears will be readied by the participant Spirit of God. This awesome sense of limitation should open us to the Spirit's help, be-

3. Dag Hammarskjöld, *Markings,* trans. W. H. Auden and Leif Sjöberg (London: Faber and Faber, 1964), 175.

4. Shirley Hazzard, "We Need Silence to Find Out What We Think," *New York Times Book Review,* November 14, 1982, 11.

cause only then can we experience the divine breakthrough by which God's rich treasures are ably served from our earthen vessels.

For many years I stood in awe of the great writers, so deeply impressed was I by their ability to cast a vision through words. They did not seem to be as restricted as I felt when they were depicting a scene of life, beckoning the reader to *see* and to react. Robertson Davies, a distinguished Canadian man of letters, wrote sometime ago about the writer's sensitivities, about how writers are encountered by circumstances in such a way that their very being is illuminated and dominated, giving their work weight and value. But when Davies went on to quote these lines of Henrik Ibsen, I was reminded that even writers feel the limits as they labor, that what they produce—however appealing and revealing—is usually less than what they had experienced as the dominating vision. Here is that statement from one of Ibsen's poems:

> To live—is a battle with troll-folk
> In the crypts of heart and head;
> To write—is a man's self-judgment
> As Doom shall judge the dead.

Self-judgment! Not even the great writers have escaped that afflicting inwardness. Yet, Davies further explained, writers cannot help being writers because the true writer does so out of an all-absorbing concern.[5] Concern is the clue to continuance, even as it is the basis of excellence.

Henry Ward Beecher's early ministry was plagued by a sickening inwardness due in large measure to his concerns over his preaching task. Most treatments of Beecher highlight his enthusiasm about everything and his great pleasure in being a public

---

5. See Robertson Davies, "The Writer's Conscience," *Saturday Review*, March 18, 1978, 42-46.

figure.[6] But there was a time during his first pastorate in Lawrenceburg, Indiana, when heavy feelings of inadequacy plagued him, so much so that he often went to bed with a headache after having preached.[7] Beecher almost left the ministry during that time of testing, but he finally found release from his problem through a deepened "consecration, solemnity, fervor, and spirituality."

What Henry Ward Beecher felt as an agony on Sunday nights, *after* having preached, John Angell James experienced on Saturday nights, just before having to preach on Sunday. R. W. Dale, James's biographer and successor as pastor of the Carr's Lane Church in Birmingham, England, explained that for many years John Angell James "scarcely ever slept on Saturday night, so uncontrollable were the apprehensions with which he looked forward to the services on Sunday."[8] Depression often followed his restlessness and uncertainty, because he thus preached without having properly slept. James sometimes canceled preaching appointments because he dreaded the way preparing for them pulled upon him inwardly. George Redford, a minister-friend, suggested that James's irritability and nervousness might not be entirely physical, that they might stem from "an excess anxiety to acquit yourself fully to your own idea of excellence and the expectations of the public, or," he further explained, "from a want of simple reliance for assistance from Him who has said He will never leave us."[9] Whatever the underlying cause for it, John Angell James for many years suffered a regular Saturday night headache as the shadow of the pulpit responsibility fell across his mind and spirit.

---

6. See Clifford E. Clark, Jr., *Henry Ward Beecher: Spokesman for a Middle-Class America* (Chicago: University of Illinois Press, 1978), chap. 5.

7. See Jane Shaffer Elsmere, *Henry Ward Beecher: The Indiana Years, 1837–1847* (Indianapolis: Indiana Historical Society, 1973), 39.

8. Robert W. Dale, ed., *The Life and Letters of John Angell James: Including an Unfinished Autobiography* (London: James Nisbet and Co., 1861), 275.

9. Ibid., 277.

Nor will we avoid that shadow—whatever its effects. The shadow will fall across every preacher's path, although we do not all experience its effects the same way. The effects of that shadow have to do with our felt limitations, our perceived needs, and our lingering fears—fear of failure, fear that we are burning out, fear that the springs of creativity have dried up—all of which can bring on panic and thwart the will to work. Søren Kierkegaard once commented that "there is nothing more dangerous for a man, nothing more paralyzing than a certain isolating self-scrutiny, in which world history, human life, society—in short, everything—disappears, and . . . in an egotistical circle one stares only at his own navel."[10] The pressure of inwardness must be released to God if ours is not to be a sickness unto death. As one of our poignant Negro Spirituals has voiced it:

> I'm troubled,
> I'm troubled,
> I'm troubled in mind,
> If Jesus don't help me
> I sho'ly will die.

A sense of inadequacy and discouraging depression can spell inward death unless these feelings are submitted to God with concern for ready assistance. Given the nature of our work, we must depend upon God, because the occasions for being frustrated are greatly increased.

The shadow of the pulpit will fall heavily across our path. It will tell us much about our needs, but it can also prod us to a deeper trust in God.

The Importance of Trust for Preaching

We must learn to live by a spirit of trust if our preaching is to be *affirmative*. True preaching is an affirmative work. The very

---

10. Gregor Malantschuk, *Kierkegaard's Thought*, ed. and trans. H. V. Hong and E. H. Hong (Princeton, N.J.: Princeton University Press, 1971), 29.

call to preach is a claim upon us to be believers, eager servants who work out of personal experience with the Lord and deep conviction about God's truth. Affirmative preaching is a declaration of salvific truth, and our inwardness stands utterly exposed in that we personally affirm it as worthy of full trust. There is always contagion and challenge when we can honestly and forthrightly share our faith in kerygmatic truth, when we can unhesitatingly promote scriptural truths as fixed, authoritative, and relevant to human need. What a difference it can make in some listeners' worldview to hear an affirmative announcement like this one: "In the beginning God created the heavens and the earth" (Gen. 1:1). What a ray of hope beams on someone's path when hearing us declare that "God is our refuge and strength,/ an ever-present help in trouble" (Ps. 46:1)! There is a ringing call to faith that sounds forth in Paul's soteric sentences: "Christ died for us" (Rom. 5:8) and "Christ Jesus came into the world to save sinners" (1 Tim 1:15*a*)! And there is a steadying assurance that grabs us when we hear the writer to the Hebrews reminding us that the Lord "is able to help those who are tempted" (Heb. 2:18) and that Christ "will appear a second time, not to bear sin, but to bring salvation to those who are waiting for him" (Heb. 9:28)! The sharing of such truths is worth all the self exposure preaching requires. After all, we can truly affirm something only as the self stands trustingly related to it.

Trust is also necessary if our preaching is to be more than mere *artistry*. The best preaching has always involved art, a high level of planning and control in the sharing of the truth. The proper matching of the *what* with the *how*, of substance with style, is a matter of personally achieved art, personal expressiveness. Suzanne K. Langer rightly commented that "all art is the creation of 'expressive forms,' or apparent forms expressive of human feelings."[11] The best preaching is both a divine word and

---

11. Suzanne K. Langer, *Problems of Art* (New York: Charles Scribner's Sons, 1957), 109.

a personal expression of it; it is a shared insight allied with a distinct, "feeling" tone. Well-planned sermons are expressive forms, self-chosen or self-created, and as such they are self-investments. As Justus George Lawler has explained: "When a man speaks an authentic word he is seeking to speak his very selfness. And since he is attempting to exteriorize his interiority, we refer to such speech as an 'uttering,' an 'outering.' "[12]

Planning and handling the form that uttering takes is what constitutes the art of preaching.[13] Those who do their planning in the spirit of loyalty to God will never be content with mere artistry; they will keep themselves open to God and the sermon surrendered to the function it should rightly serve. Mere artistry in the pulpit is a product of vain self-love; it is a selfish attempt to hide an exposed self behind the fig leaves of rhetoric or vain drama.

The honest preacher knows, and cannot forget, that sermons are only means, and never ends in themselves. That preacher also chafes under the awareness that rarely, if ever, does a sermon, however well planned, do full justice to the text that stimulated thought and stirred the soul. We all do well to be content with the fact that despite any sermonic prowess on our part, our sermons always end up as weak carriers of the initial vision of the truth, as something far less than the grand, living

12. Justus George Lawler, *The Christian Image: Studies in Religious Art and Poetry* (Pittsburgh: Duquesne University Press, 1966), 11.

13. Many studies of homiletics deal with preaching as an art. The following titles, both ancient and modern, are just a few illustrative works: W. Perkins, *The Art of Prophesying* (Cambridge: John Legatt, 1612–13); W. Chappell, *The Preacher and the Art and Method of Preaching (Methodus Concionandi)* (London, 1651); E. C. Dargan, *The Art of Preaching in the Light of Its History* (New York: George H. Doran, 1922); Charles Reynolds Brown, *The Art of Preaching* (New York: Macmillan, 1922); Charles Smyth, *The Art of Preaching* (London: SPCK, 1940); Leslie J. Tizard, *Preaching: The Art of Communication* (London: Allen & Unwin, 1958); Lionel Crocker, ed., *Harry Emerson Fosdick's Art of Preaching: An Anthology* (Springfield, Ill.: Charles C. Thomas, 1971); Henry H. Mitchell, *Black Preaching: Recovery of a Powerful Art* (Nashville: Abingdon Press, 1990).

insight. We will spend our lives forever working to make our statements better servants of truth, and in doing so we will be forever trying to turn our insides out. This is the reality of our lot, the agony that attends whatever ecstasy we sometimes enjoy. It is quite sobering to be forever busy studying our craft, examining and rehearsing the creative process, isolating and rejoining the elements of good speechmaking, all in the attempt to apply ourselves more aptly for a more effective pulpit experience.

Our concern to be better in the pulpit is quite evident in the way we buy and study books about preaching—and even the sermons of other preachers. There are those who not only *read* those sermons but *raid* them as well—but in vain, because the best preaching always exacts a personal involvement in what we say. Always there seems some elusive aspect to our work, some secret of success that hides itself from view. So we probe what others have written about preaching, and we pore over famous sermons, always seeking, reaching, questing. Sometimes we are privileged to hear other preachers preach and to interrogate them about their work, only to feel more inward sensitivity when we realize that what we saw, heard, and felt in that preacher's presence was something more than he or she could explain.

Donald Macleod, emeritus professor of preaching at Princeton Theological Seminary, some years ago compiled and published the descriptions of pulpit preparation from thirteen acknowledged pulpit masters, together with a sample sermon from each one. The book was titled *Here Is My Method,* and its appearance in print was in response to a request from many preachers who had heard and admired those thirteen pastors.[14] The preachers who requested such a book wanted to learn from those they considered masters, anxious to gain insight for greater pulpit aptness. Clarence Stonelynn Roddy prepared and published

---

14. Donald Macleod, ed., *Here Is My Method: The Art of Sermon Construction* (Westwood, N.J. : Fleming H. Revell, 1952).

a similar volume highlighting a different group of preachers for study.[15] Both sets of preachers shared their testimony, and their secrets—but only in part. The full secret of effective pulpit work involves more than training and talent. It involves mysterious and individual factors, a personal application of the self, and the harnessing of what is inward through consecration and spirituality.

There can be something other in our pulpit work than mere artistry. There can be perspective, proportion, focused vision, and a contagious "feeling" tone. A God-harnessed inwardness can create its own expressive forms and convey contagious overtones of mediated Presence. Preaching does expose us, but we need not try to hide behind the word walls we build only for display. It has pleased God to be revealed in the awesome exposure of God's servants as they preach.

In his *Confessions,* Augustine recalled at one point his young years with the Manichaens and how utterly disappointed he had been with one of the teachers, who had proved unable to answer Augustine's pressing questions. The teacher was fluent, eloquent, and artistic in speech, but Augustine commented, "But of what profit to me was the elegance of my cup-bearer, since he offered me not the more precious draught for which I thirsted?"[16] Although preaching is by nature an artful self-expression, we must not preach with art in mind but with lives in view. Constantine Stanislavski used to caution his student actors: "You have to like the art in you, not yourself in the art."[17]

Michael Polanyi wrote something along this line with respect to the effective use of tools: that we gain freedom in using them

15. See Clarence S. Roddy, ed., *We Prepare and Preach: The Practice of Sermon Construction and Delivery* (Chicago: Moody Press, 1959).

16. Augustine, *Confessions,* book 6, trans. J. G. Pilkington (New York: Heritage Press, 1963), 67-68.

17. Cited by Helen Drees Ruttencutter, *Pianist's Progress* (New York: Thomas Y. Crowell, 1979), 68.

only when our attention shifts from their use to the result they help us to achieve. He called this the difference between "subsidiary awareness and focal awareness."[18] We are freed up to preach with power only as our attention moves away from the anxious self to consider the end we seek through our work. Intentionality must prevail as we preach. The concern must not be inward but outward; the focus must not be on the self as speaking servant, or on the sermon as the medium or tool, but on the purpose, on the *what* and the *why* of preaching. Polanyi further explained that tools are effectively used only when "we pour ourselves out into them and assimilate them as parts of our own existence."[19]

Drawing Strength from a "Call" to Preach

I once heard Gardner Taylor say, while lecturing to ministers, that "one of our chief problems as preachers is finding enough inner security, by God's grace, to do our work without being intimidated by the society around us, and without trying to court the favor of people who are in power." He said this while talking about perils preachers face in doing their work. It is in the strength of a divinely given call to preach that the preacher will rightly deal with the concern for "enough inner security."

A genuine experience of a divinely given call to preach is one of the factors that assist us to bear the burdens associated with the pulpit experience. The pulpit task is an immense one; it is so overwhelming that no human being naturally possesses the resources demanded to fulfill it. In speaking about a "call" to preach, I am referring to a realized experience of having been chosen by God for the task, a remembered encounter that marks out the receiving person's identity and involvement as a

18. Michael Polanyi, *Personal Knowledge* (Chicago: University of Chicago Press, 1958), 55-56.
19. Ibid.

preacher. Being called to preach involves an understanding that God has addressed us personally about the use of our life, although the experience of being so addressed does not happen to everyone in just the same way. But however one is initially aware of that call, at least five crucial features can be isolated regarding what it does and means.

1. Being called to preach is an experience that places a demand upon us, and the result is a convictional knowledge about an assignment. When God addresses us, by whatever means and in whatever context, we experience either a sense of opportunity or a demand. In some cases, the call taps a prior interest on our part, or it can generate a new interest that surpasses other interests to which we had been giving attention.

I speak here about a "convictional knowledge" because being called to preach is a convictional experience. James E. Loder has offered this helpful description of such knowledge: "At the heart of convictional knowing is a radical figure-ground shift that is not merely perceptual but existential, in which the truth of Christ's revelation transforms the subject from a knower into one who is fully known and comprehended by what he or she first knew. . . . The essence of convictional knowing is the intimacy of the self with its Source."[20]

2. The call guides us in a challenging direction that becomes central to our new identity, beliefs, and behavior. The call links us more intimately with God, with the added understanding that we are identified with the divine will in a particular way.

3. The call is an experience that aids our self-development, granting us a point for integrating the self. A call acquaints us not only with a sensed responsibility, but also with a sense of opportunity and an arena of giftedness. Contemplating these

---

20. James E. Loder, *The Transforming Moment: Understanding Convictional Experiences* (San Francisco: Harper & Row, 1981), 122-23.

opportunities and surrendering ourselves to them helps us to give the self a primary focus.

4. The experience of receiving a call from God to preach grants us a new surge of life. It grants a plus to our normal energies and natural powers. As Howard Thurman once explained it, "When a man is able to bring to bear upon a single purpose all the powers of his being, his whole life is energized and vitalized."[21] He added, "At such a moment he knows what, in the living of his life, he must be *for* and what he must be against."[22]

5. Staying surrendered to the demands and opportunities for which the call is given opens new springs of creativity within us. Rollo May has suggested that "creativity occurs in an act of encounter and is to be understood with this encounter as its center."[23]

The person who accepts "chosenness" for pulpit ministry moves from the time and point of the call into the time of specific conditioning for the role. This conditioning is necessary to make us ready for effective work. The conditioning will involve living through personal crises, developing healthy attitudes, maturing emotionally, gaining a useful body of knowledge, gaining wisdom from convictional experiences, and, among many other experiences and benefits, handling assignments under the guidance of mentors.

In many church bodies, a prescribed period of seminary study is required before one can receive a regular pulpit assignment. It is a mandated time during which one must remain under the tutelage of approved scholars commissioned to map out and monitor students' learning processes. By means of a measured set of formal studies, together with supervised field work, semi-

---

21. Howard Thurman, *Disciplines of the Spirit* (New York: Harper & Row, 1963), 19.
22. Ibid., 34.
23. Rollo May, *The Courage to Create* (New York: W. W. Norton, 1975), 77.

narians are finally certified as having met the formational and informational standards traditionally required to gain standing as ordained clergy. Honoring benchmarks set long ago for theological education in the United States, and with continuing close attention to the perceived needs of the church in our time, the fourfold curriculum pattern of an accredited seminary is of such scope that a student needs at least three years to complete it.

This educational process, and the ongoing demand for it, reflects a wisdom accumulated within the wider church across several centuries; and we know that it is the most formal and systematic way to make someone ready to preach. But let us never make the mistake of believing that this educational process is sufficient in itself to grant preaching readiness. Given the burdensome nature and eternal purpose of the preaching task, nothing less than a divinely given call to engage in it is adequate to inform us about its importance, to strengthen us for its demands, or to keep us encouraged to remain at it in the midst of great stress.

I have dealt with the preacher's initiating experience of a call in only brief fashion, but there are some longer and more detailed studies that treat the experience in fuller fashion. *The Irresistible Urge to Preach,* by William H. Myers, is one of them, along with the companion volume by him, entitled *God's Yes Was Louder Than My No.*[24] The first volume presents the "call" stories of eighty-six preachers, all African Americans, all nationally known, and some known internationally known, based on Myers's interviews of them. In the companion volume, Myers breaks fresh ground by using cross-disciplinary research skills to bring multiple perspectives to bear upon the call stories

---

24. William H. Myers, *The Irresistible Urge to Preach: A Collection of African American "Call" Stories* (Atlanta: Aaron Press, 1992); and *God's Yes Was Louder Than My No: Rethinking the African American Call to Ministry* (Grand Rapids: Eerdmans, 1994).

reported in the earlier study. After treating the call experience from the perspective of story and narrative (in which the preachers reported on the struggle, the search, the sanction, and the surrender resulting from the experience), Myers explores their call experiences as rites of passage and examines hermeneutical and cultural factors associated with these experiences. I urge a study of these works, because Myers's research, though based on experiences of African American preachers only, actually offers basic insights for persons from any racial or ethnic setting who seek a greater understanding of the phenomenon of a call to preach.

I must be personal for a moment. I want to report that I did not choose the preaching ministry; it was chosen for me. I was summoned to it through an experience of call that is still as fresh in my memory now, at this telling, as when it all first happened. It was an experience that has been indispensible for my sense of direction and inner security as I have sought to honor God and maintain my footing in the sometimes turbulent waters of the preaching task.

I had planned to be a musician, not a minister. All the signs along the path of my interest pointed to a career as a pianist, not as a preacher. But it was not to be so, and for reasons that point back straight to God.

My experience of call happened on a Sunday morning. I was at church, part of the congregation engaged in worship. The morning worship service was in progress, but my attention was divided. I was aware of the progress of the service, but was paying more attention to a music score I had brought with me to study. I often carried some music score with me when away from home, intent on using any available moment to examine the notation for structure, phrasing, and problems, to ease the memorization process. That day I had with me the score of a waltz by Chopin.

During a brief let-up in my concentration on that waltz, I

found myself captured by the spirit of the worship occasion. As I honored the meaning of that hour and opened myself to God, I felt caught up in an almost transfixed state, and I heard a Voice speaking within my consciousness: "I want you to preach!"

It was a strange but sure happening. The Voice both disturbed me and settled me. The message was so forceful, and the meaning was distinct and clear. I knew I would have to say yes!

Still in the grip of the encounter, I turned to the person sitting next to me. In the uprush of my feelings, I interrupted her worship. Feeling the necessity to announce the news about my new direction, I asked her, "Do you know what I am going to do with my life?" The interruption was perhaps excusable, because she was one of the more serious believers within our youth fellowship, but the interrupting question I asked was hardly appropriate, for how could she know until I told her? But the desire to tell her was the reason for the interruption! She understood that, and politely replied, "No, James. What?" I softly but decidedly said, "I'm going to be a preacher!" Her reply was just as forthright, and she gave an affirming smile as she voiced it: "Why, James, that is *wonderful!*"

It was all so graphic to my inner sight, and so gripping upon my mind and spirit. The Voice that called me was so clear, and its bidding, though gentle, bore the unmistakable authority of a higher realm. I had a new direction and a duty for which to prepare. I also had a problem. The new direction I was given put me into an identity crisis, since I had been so deeply involved in preparing to be a concert pianist. Thus began a prolonged and painful process by which I was inwardly sifted, learning at a deeper level how to submit my will and plans to what I now understood as God's sovereign plan for me.[25]

More than fifty years have transpired since that holy hour of

---

25. For a fuller account and assessment of Massey's experience of call, see Myers, *The Irresistible Urge to Preach*, 230-32; and Myers, *God's Yes Was Louder Than My No*, 30-31, 49, 244, 261.

call. They have been years filled with pondering and preaching, searching and finding, gaining and losing, years of mountaintop experiences and journeys through the valleys and jungles of life. But I have been sustained through it all by the meaning and momentum gained from listening and yielding during that great moment of grace. Since that time of experienced call, I have known with surety the work to which my head, heart, and hands were to be devoted. And knowing that has made all the difference in my life and my labors!

CHAPTER TWO

The Outward Side of Preaching

Having looked briefly at the inward and personal side of the pulpit experience, we now turn to look at aspects of its public side, at what I here term the *outward* side of preaching. Charles R. Brown was referring to that outward side when, writing about the preacher at work, he commented: "If he is really preaching you *hear* him, you *see* him, you *feel* him!"[1] Good and great preaching have distinct, salient marks at four levels: the perceptions the preacher evokes, the meaning the preacher mediates, the style the preacher adopts, and the involvement the preacher generates. All of these are part of the outward side of what we seek to do through the pulpit, part of what the gathered people perceive from our work.

Perceptions Preaching Should Evoke

Those to whom we preach will perceive something from our pulpit presence and work. If we rightly harness our inwardness, the people should surely perceive our honest interest in their welfare.

---

1. Charles R. Brown, *The Art of Preaching* (New York: Macmillan, 1922), 27, italics added.

Blessed is the preacher who so speaks as to assure all hearers that God knows and loves each one, that even though facing a crowd, God always has the individual in mind. This can be done, however large and heterogeneous the mass of people before us. It happens more surely when we remember our mutual involvement with hearers in the common ventures of life, when we address people in the light of the divine concern and our own honest openness to aid them. It happens when people perceive that we are not just engaged in a professional task but serve with a personal commitment stirred by love. It happens when hearers sense that we are not only text-oriented but person-minded as well. To be sure, there are text-oriented preachers whose chief concern seems focused upon a strict delineation of biblical meanings with very little, if any, tie-in with human interest or situational need. And there are task-oriented preachers who seem so bent on getting their work done that they appear aloof from people for whom their ministry was ordained. The salient mark of caring is still necessary to bring preacher and people together in trust. No preaching succeeds like that done by a warm-hearted, open, and concerned preacher, someone with whom hearers can identify with no fear or suspicion of calculated openness.

Alexander Whyte once reported a woman's comment to her minister on one occasion: " 'Sir, your preaching does my soul good.' And her minister never forgot the grave and loving look with which that was said."[2] Not only did that preacher remember those warm words, but often when selecting what to preach, his heart and conscience always asked him, "Will that do my friend's soul any good?" No preaching succeeds like that prepared and delivered with an honest interest in doing what is good for the hearer.

---

2. Alexander Whyte, *Bunyan's Characters* (Philadelphia: Presbyterian Board of Education and Sabbath-School Work, 1893), 87.

There is a rule by which human helpfulness happens. It is the rule of thinking of others, and not just of oneself. There is a word from Paul about this grand rule: "Do nothing out of selfish ambition or vain conceit. . . . Each of you should look not only to your own interests, but also to the interests of others. Your attitude should be the same as that of Christ Jesus" (Phil. 2:3-5). Those who would preach must by all means follow this rule.

Booker T. Washington, the noted African American who gained honor as a social leader and educator during the post-Reconstruction period, mentioned in his autobiography how his life had been filled with many great and encouraging surprises, many of them due, as he told it, to his effort "to make every day reach as nearly as possible the high-water mark of pure, unselfish, useful living."[3] Washington made that comment in a section of his story written to honor those who had assisted him in securing what was necessary to create, develop, and support Tuskegee Institute, the now-famous university he founded and guided until his untimely death. Washington was grateful to the many benefactors, advisers, and encouragers who had looked and thought beyond themselves to help him and those for whom he did his thinking and work. The will to care and share is the first step toward human benefit at any level of life and endeavor.

The apostle Paul understood and advocated the rule of thinking unselfishly, and the reports we have about his life and ministry well illustrate that he lived by such a rule. His word to the Philippians, just stated, was a reminder from him to continue their unselfish regard for each other. He wrote to them from prison, expecting to be released and to rejoin them in due time; but he knew that the congregation could endure and remain a vital people even in his continued absence if they remained true to the rules for church progress through unselfish regard and full

---

3. See Booker T. Washington, *Up From Slavery: An Autobiography* (1901; reprint, Garden City, N.Y.: Doubleday, 1953), 293.

sharing. *Each of you should look not only to your own interests, but also to the interests of others.*

This rule by which Christian experience and church life go forward is the same rule by which preaching accomplishes its intended end. Actually, this rule explains the way Jesus Christ became the suffering servant God used to bring deliverance within reach to a fallen human race. Thus that hymn of praise to Christ that Paul penned in Philippians 2:6-11. It is the grandest illustration Paul could offer of unselfish caring. There, in a fresh form, in a lyrical hymn, Paul restated the gospel and celebrated anew the Christ-event. The statement is short but supremely substantive. It places the Incarnation in full view. There, in a two-part movement, is a song about Christ—his Incarnation as Son (what was involved, why it happened), and his resultant exaltation as Lord (why it happened and what will follow from it in due time). The passage stirs one to imitate the example set by our Lord. It tells us to live by "his mind," by his unselfish way of thinking. In the light of this, John Watson, the noted English preacher, declared, "Altruism is written in everlasting and resplendent character on the Cross of Christ, and it was at Calvary that the centre of life shifted from selfishness to sacrifice."[4] Unselfish caring is a trait every preacher must seek to cultivate, learning to give time and attention to others and their needs. Opening ourselves to live by such a rule is something of which we are capable, and remembering the purpose of our work in the world can stir us to do so with readiness and without fear. Only in this way can we plan and share what is always good for the hearer, and ensure that our preaching will be the vitalizing, strengthening influence that it should be.

I shall not soon forget hearing preacher Gardner C. Taylor tell about an experience of relationship generated in part by his

---

4. See John Watson [Ian Maclaren], *Respectable Sins* (London: Hodder & Stoughton, 1909), 236.

preaching. The close relationship was with a devoted deacon in the Concord Baptist Church when Taylor was pastor there. The deacon was a man who always received the preaching in the same spirit of warmth that he perceived in it. On the day before the good deacon died, Pastor Taylor visited him in the intensive care unit of the hospital. The deacon was now comatose. His daughter sat at the bedside, remembering what had been the last words she had heard him speak. Knowing the deacon's love for his pastor, the daughter told Taylor, "The last thing I remember him saying was 'I wish I could hear him preach one more time!' "[5] That deacon had perceived from that preacher an honest interest in his welfare. The result was an eager hearing of the preacher's word and a valued partnership in church life.

Those to whom we preach should perceive *our sense of partnership with them in life and witness.*

There is nothing that stirs one to serious pulpit service like the warmth and favor of what T. W. Rumsby explained as "a voluntary, agreed and convenanted understanding between the congregation which calls their own minister and the minister who receives and accepts that call."[6] A warm relationship between preacher and people is crucial to a meaningful and treasured pulpit experience. It is no small matter for people to "sit under" our preaching, with us literally above them in a raised section of the sanctuary and figuratively above them in the sense of that over/under arrangement between leader and followers. But whether in symbolism or in actual fact, those who "sit under" us can often determine the extent to which we feel happy in our work or harassed by it.

Leslie J. Tizard, speaking at a gathering in London's West-

5. Gardner C. Taylor, *How Shall They Preach?* (Elgin, Ill.: Progressive Baptist Publishing House, 1977), 93.

6. T. W. Rumsby, "Leslie Tizard as Minister and Preacher," in *Facing Life and Death: In Commemoration of the Late Rev. Leslie J. Tizard*, ed. Harry Guntrip (London: George Allen and Unwin, Ltd., 1959), 19.

minster Chapel in 1952, fours years before his untimely death, told about how he had to learn proper focus for fellowship in preaching. When he was a student, he confessed, he had fantasies of himself spending long, long hours in the cloistered seclusion of a study, writing sermons he would deliver with breathtaking eloquence to admiring crowds of listeners. He did not at that time think he would like pastoral work, a service he thought of as "fussing around people." But once in the pastorate, he learned the strength and beauty that are to be found in shared life and witness. Actually, his first ministry setting was a dockland area where there were poverty and dire unemployment, so that he came into contact with life in the raw. Still confessing, the now-seasoned preacher reported: "In one way and another it dawned upon me that I should never be able to preach in any way that mattered if I did not in some measure know and understand the fears and anxieties, the sins and follies, the frustrations and failures of men."[7]

Partnership in the common ventures of life gives preacher and people a common understanding of human need and an openness to divine help. Preaching proceeds best not from correct and fluent exegesis alone, but from a sensed camaraderie with the people in the need for grace and the hope of God's glory.

In his autobiography, *With Head and Heart,* Howard Thurman tells about a pulpit failure during his first pastorate in Oberlin, Ohio. The failure was trying to pack too much into his sermons—the zeal of which offended the sensibilities of his hearers. Thurman reported, "And they did not hesitate to let me know it."[8] The church members were right; they were seeking an honorable partnership, a needed togetherness, an honest and supportive relationship. An open and concerned person, Thurman learned from the people, adapted in keeping with their

---

7. Leslie J. Tizard, "The Work of the Ministry," in ibid., 37-38.
8. Howard Thurman, *With Head and Heart: The Autobiography of Howard Thurman* (New York: Harcourt, Brace, Jovanovich, 1979), 66.

wisdom, and engendered their trust to learn from him. That he went on to become one of the greatest preachers this country has known is now common knowledge.[9]

Theologian Martin E. Marty commented in print that in all of his years of preaching (ten in the pastorate with weekly pulpit duties) and across the succeeding years in and out of other pulpits, "I have been moved to learn something: the message has greatest effect when it is most clear that the people with whom I am a hearer are participating in preaching . . . [that] they are 'preaching *with*' [the preacher]."[10] A true partnership in intent worship can generate a trust that aids the reception of proclaimed truth.

The Preacher as Fellow Worshiper

Something is being perceived as we preach, and our bearing as a worshiper will aid or hinder that perception.

Lawyer-churchman George Wharton Pepper, one of the few non-clerics to give the Lyman Beecher Lectures at Yale Divinity School, shared with those attending there in 1914 his views of how preachers are perceived from the pew during worship. In one declarative passage, Pepper explained: "Speaking for myself, I am powerfully affected by the bearing of a man during service time. I find that, if he reads from the Bible, a great deal can be gathered respecting his inner self."[11]

Pepper then warned against doing that reading with an affected solemnity or in a "scripture voice" that is clearly different from one's regular voice. He confessed utter disappointment when the reading showed no perceived difference between the

---

9. In the April 6, 1953 issue of *Life* magazine, the board of judges listed Howard Thurman as one of the twelve greatest preachers in the United States.

10. Martin E. Marty, *The Word: People Participating in Preaching* (Philadelphia: Fortress Press, 1984), 19.

11. George Wharton Pepper, *A Voice From the Crowd* (New Haven, Conn.: Yale University Press, 1915), 8-9.

low and the high passages in the Bible. Then after stating that a preacher's prayers also reveal the level of her or his personal reverence, Pepper stressed that the people in the pews expect a preacher's reverence to be felt in what is done. "You will ask me, perhaps, what I mean by reverence," he stated. "It is not a manner or tone or a posture. It is something the effect of which is confined to the [preacher]. . . . I am inclined to describe it as the atmosphere exhaled by a [person] who is aware of the Presence of God."[12] These were the words of a noted and perceptive lay churchman about the outward aspects of pulpit ministry.

Those who experience our pulpit ministry will perceive something in connection with us. Will they perceive a caring that includes them? Will they perceive an evident scholarship, richly blended with deep reverence? Will they sense both a love for truth and a warmth for persons—a spirit of inclusiveness reflected in the conscious use of non-sexist language? When we stand to preach, we *show* something along with what we *say*. We cause our hearers to *feel* as well as *hear* something. What will it be?

Frank W. Boreham was a boy when Dwight L. Moody visited England to preach there. Boreham went with his father to one of the outdoor services, and the two were fortunate to gain a spot within just a few feet of the platform, where they could see and hear Moody very well. Young Frank was happily surprised that he could understand every word Moody spoke. Looking back on that experience many years later, Boreham wrote: "I had assumed that preachers of eminence must be very abstruse, recondite, and difficult to follow. I hoped that, by intense concentration, I might occasionally catch the drift of the speaker's argument." But, fortunately, that had not been the case, because Moody preached using "the simplest and most homely speech,"

---

12. Ibid., 11.

Boreham explained, adding, "He told stories that interested and affected me . . . he held my attention spellbound until the last syllable died away. . . . It was all so different—so delightfully different—from what I had expected the utterance of a world-renowned preacher to be."[13]

While we must admit that more than one factor was involved in the young boy's enthrallment by Moody's preaching, it must be said that Dwight L. Moody never forgot the outward side of his pulpit work. Moody knew its inwardness all too well, and he chafed over it, as all sensitive preachers do. But he worked hard at his craft, always eager that his message be perceived rightly and his ministry accepted. Robert W. Dale, a well-seasoned preacher, was also impressed by Moody's preaching and joyously worked along with him in the evangelical mission there. Dale's positive comments about Moody's preaching confirm that its outward side was richly helpful.[14]

The Preacher as Anointed Servant

In treating the outward side of our pulpit work, there is one more aspect that I must mention here: the sense of divine anointing our preaching should carry and convey. We who preach not only *present* a message, but also *represent* its Sender.

The pulpit ministry can make a world of difference for our hearers when we are perceived as being on God's mission, not our own, when it seems forcefully clear that our being in such a service role involves something more than a personal choice. True preaching readiness is by divine appointment to the task, and a distinct anointing for it is one of the credentials that certify our readiness and right to preach.

---

13. Frank W. Boreham, *My Pilgrimage: An Autobiography* (Philadelphia: Judson Press, 1950), 51-52.

14. See A. W. W. Dale, *The Life of R. W. Dale of Birmingham* (London: Hodder & Stoughton, 1898), esp. 318-20.

Our way as spiritual leaders is marked out for us by two basic influences: nature and grace. The influence of nature is seen in our personality, intellect, temperament, and natural gifts. The influence of grace—that is, the favor God has evidenced to us—is seen in the way the touch of God upon our lives has harnessed and enhanced those natural factors so that we have been made ready to serve God. As preachers we are responsible to deal with the things of God and speak about them, so that as we speak and act God is present and active in it all. This is what divine anointing is all about.

The concept of anointed service or an anointed selfhood reflects four distinct features. I have written more fully on this in a previous book, but a brief summary is in order here.[15]

1. There is a sense of assertiveness by which one can readily act.
2. There is a gripping knowledge that one is identified with God's will in that action.
3. There is an intensity to what one does, because one's actions are related to a higher frame of reference.
4. There is a decisive "instinctiveness" for what is being done.

The New Testament speaks of Jesus as one "anointed" by God (Luke 4:18; Acts 10:38), and the accounts always link his service with the fact that he was appointed by God to do what he was doing. Luke's interest in the theme of anointing is readily seen throughout his writings, and it was Luke who preserved for us our Lord's own use of Isaiah 6:1-2 as the apt description of his directedness and authority:

---

15. See James Earl Massey, *The Sermon in Perspective: A Study of Communication and Charisma* (Grand Rapids: Baker Book House and Warner Press, 1976), esp. 101-6. See also James Forbes, *The Holy Spirit and Preaching,* the Lyman Beecher Lectures on Preaching 1986 (Nashville: Abingdon Press, 1989), esp. 53-65.

"The Spirit of the Lord is on me,
because he has anointed me
to preach good news to the poor."
(Luke 4:18a)

Did not Luke highlight this theme of anointing in treating the life and work of the preachers listed in the Acts of the Apostles? Is this not a requisite for every spiritual leader? As servants of the same Lord, we have no independent power or integrity. We who preach must find our life and effectiveness under the creative touch of an enabling, anointing God. The New Testament writers used the descriptive terms *charisma,* "divine giftedness," and *chrisma,* "anointing," for such enabling. Both terms point decisively to the work of God in the life of a human being, a work linked not with mere ritual but with a responding self entrusted with an appointed mission. Preaching is such a mission.

James S. Stewart understood how the wondrous experience of being divinely claimed for service gives content and contagion to our selfhood and service. In his Beecher Lectures at Yale in 1952, he said to the preachers and seminarians gathered before him: "In particular, let the Christian preacher, the herald of the good news of God, think of his own life being interpenetrated with the very life of Jesus."[16] Stewart went on to add:

We are apt in these days to be besieged by life's unbearable enigmas and battered by its frightening responsibilities. . . . We tell ourselves it is absurd that we should even attempt to be Christ's witnesses in a world like this and with a nature like our own: for "who is sufficient for these things?" And then across our hectic fever falls the voice of calm: "Lo, I am with you alway, even unto the end"; and we know that, whatever happens, He is

---

16. James S. Stewart, *A Faith to Proclaim,* the Lyman Beecher Lectures on Preaching 1952 (New York: Charles Scribner's Sons, 1953), 157.

quite certain to be there. This is the way to peace, and to the consciousness of adequate resources.[17]

This is why an anointing from God is imperative for our work as preachers. The "adequate resources" it makes available to us are the validating marks of Christ's presence with us.

The call to preach and the benefits of an anointing must be understood as related in our work. The following chart might help to make this relation clear:

The Relation Between Call and Anointing	
Features of the Call	*Factors of Anointing*
1. A convictional knowledge of God's claim upon one's life.	
2. A sense of focused identity.	1. A sense of being identified with God's will in relating to some need.
3. A sense of purpose that integrates the self for action.	
4. A sense of harnessed energies.	2. A sense of assertiveness by which to act.
5. A heightened creativity.	3. A sense of "instinct" for relating to what needs to be done.

This anointing of which I speak is usually sensed by our hearers through an authority that attends our work. Our day, we are repeatedly told, is a day of eroded authority, both religious and civic. As for the erosion of authority in religious matters, some blame this partly on changing views about the nature and relevance of Scripture, partly on the loss of confidence in the church as a valid agency for social transformation, and partly on the ineptitude of preaching as a viable form of communication.

17. Ibid., 158.

If there is an authority to attend our pulpit work, then what kind is it?

For one thing, we preach by *derived authority*, by a God-given right to speak. As Romans 10:15*a* tells us, "And how can they preach unless they are sent?" Next, that authority to preach is a *shared authority*. We who preach are sharers in a spiritual community, and we bear credentials as ordained (authorized) persons who are endorsed by and accountable to that spiritual community in whose life and heritage we share. Yet again, our authority as preachers issues from the scriptural truths that determine our message. Still another authority factor is *spiritual experience,* that observable evidence in character, wisdom, and contagion when one is living a God-oriented life. All these factors are involved in the anointing and authority a pulpit ministry should carry and convey.

My youth took place during a period when the service of preaching was highly respected, and even romanticized. The fact that I grew up within the black church setting no doubt deepened my respect for the preaching task, because it was considered a high privilege to be a "called" person, to be able to confess and confirm the Lord's touch upon one's life to speak for God. My father and grandfather were working preachers, so even the home circle blessed my perceptions of the preaching ministry as, indeed, a high calling. Sometime after I experienced a call to the preaching ministry, I began to sense the demands that attend it: familiarity with the biblical materials, an understanding of the human condition, insight into the communication process, a love for people, and a sustained openness to God in prayerful obedience. There are still other demands to be met for an approved ministry, such as a loving commitment to preach. This also is a perceived element of pulpit power. It was said of the world-famous pianist Arthur Rubinstein, when he was still playing vigorously in recitals at age seventy-five, "He loves what he is doing, and communicates his love to the audience. The audience reciprocates."[18] The same law operates in pulpit work. When we love God, love God's truth, love people, and love what we have been divinely called to do for their spiritual and human needs, then our service will emit an attractive essence and an authoritative glow.

At a time when it is true that no voice remains unchallenged, we must remember that many of our hearers will honestly question some truth we proclaim or some tradition we represent; and many will exercise their freedom against being regimented by an authority we exercise. While some preachers might view this as a curse, it can be treated positively as an occasion for love to win its way. This is why we must love people as well as the truth we seek to share. That love for them will help us inwardly and outwardly, enabling us to be patient rather than pushy, ardent but not argumentative, persistent but not cantankerous, prophetic but also pastoral. In the final analysis, the preaching that will make the right difference proceeds out of love.

18. See Harold C. Schonberg, *Facing the Music* (New York: Summit Books, 1981), 326-27. The comment was from a newspaper review Schonberg gave in 1964, a few days before Rubinstein's seventy-fifth birthday.

CHAPTER THREE

Achieving Togetherness Through Preaching

Christian preaching fulfills itself by shaping a community in which Christ is the living center and within which persons relate meaningfully through his love. Preaching at its best involves persons in relation, and to encourage this result the preaching must be both personal and pertinent. There is something most contagious and inviting about our preaching when those who are hearing us sense that we truly regard them and have their best interests as our motivating concern. The miracle of community happens within the rich context of sharing, when both the preacher and the hearers match in eagerness, earnestness, trust, openness, and regard. All of this is included in the experience of togetherness, which this chapter treats.

Preaching and the Vision of Community

We who preach must deal simultaneously on two fronts while in the pulpit: (1) We must deal, as I have said earlier, with that personal front of our own inward reactions, seeking to keep the whole self harnessed for a focused service; and (2) we must deal with the public front, reaching out in concern toward all those we are addressing on God's behalf. Interestingly, if we succeed well on that personal front, the people will experience our presence as the contagious sharing of ourselves. The fact is that our hearers usually deepen in their listening in relation to how we deepen in self-giving as we speak. Another way of putting it is to say that we who preach must bring to the task and offer to our hearers a full self if we are eager to touch other lives.

Human togetherness is a vital concern to God, and the public side of the pulpit experience is a part of the divine strategy to effect and further that togetherness. The preacher is sent to bring persons into an accepting togetherness with God and with each other, through shared truths that make God's will known. The sermon, therefore, must be engagingly clear, and the preacher must be expressively focused and personal in sharing its truths. Togetherness between preacher and hearers demands a rightly focused speaker and listeners who give a full and eager hearing. Douglas V. Steere treated the dynamics of listening in one of his seminal books, asking, "Have you ever talked with someone who listened with such utter abandon to what you were trying to tell him that you were yourself made clearer in what you were trying to express by the very quality of his listening?"[1] Think about this with reference to the way some persons respond so avidly to preaching, and you will readily understand what I mean by an experience of "togetherness" between preacher and hearers. Steere asked his question with an interest in personal conversation, but what he highlighted as "utter and easy attentiveness" and "free and open listening" applies equally to the preaching/listening event as well. It does happen more often when the preacher remains open, personal, and pertinent and regards others while preaching.

But allied with personal openness on our part needs to be a basis for the hearers to trust us. It is incumbent upon those who preach to nurture such trust by evidencing honesty, integrity, and

---

1. Douglas V. Steere, *On Listening to Another* (New York: Harper and Bros., 1955), 1.

a solemn faithfulness to the task. Paul once declared that his life was free from the shameful things that one hides, and that he refused "to use deception, nor do we distort the word of God. On the contrary, by setting forth the truth plainly we commend ourselves to every man's conscience in the sight of God" (2 Cor. 4:2). There are clear principles that need to govern our calling, and adhering to those principles will allow us to be open before the people, with no cause for shame because there is no sham. We who preach can have confidence as we do our work, and by our deeds and demeanor we can grant a basis to others for confidence in receiving our work.

Paul's word about honesty and openness on the part of the preacher should be understood to mean that there must be no separation in our lives between how we live and how we labor.[2] Because of the nature and scope of the preacher's calling, both life and work must be harnessed to express it all. The preacher's work should make the foundational calling evident, while the preacher's life should be an instance of experienced grace. This understanding is crucial for a proper pulpit ministry, because it lets our preaching be heard and trusted as an honest public response to God, on the one hand, and as an honest reaching out to our hearers, on the other hand. If such an understanding sustains us, we who preach will be able to do our proper work not as celebrities but as celebrants, calling attention strictly and steadily to God and Christ. Therefore, Paul went on to confess, "We do not preach ourselves, but Jesus Christ as Lord, and ourselves as your servants for Jesus' sake" (2 Cor. 4:5). Those who listen to preaching experience both the proclamation being spoken and the speaking proclaimer at one and the same time.

---

2. On the 2 Corinthians 4:1-15 passage, see Rudolf Bultmann, *The Second Letter to the Corinthians*, ed. and trans. Roy A. Harrisville (Minneapolis: Augsburg, 1985), 98-102; Victor Paul Furnish, *II Corinthians: A Commentary*, Anchor Bible Commentary (Garden City, N.Y.: Doubleday, 1984), esp. 217-20, 245-50; and Ralph P. Martin, *Second Corinthians*, Word Biblical Commentary (Waco: Word Books, 1986), 74-81.

It is basic to the calling that there be a perceived togetherness between what is spoken and the one who speaks, because both the message and the messenger should be accepted by the hearer. Only in this way can that fuller togetherness happen for which the divine plan for preaching was enacted.

Preaching is a divinely appointed way to gain and nurture community—that togetherness lived in celebration of God. The late Samuel D. Proctor busied himself for many years summoning the churches and the nation to embrace and embody "genuine community." He explained that we need something deep, durable, and genuine if we are to be in community as God desires, with each and all marked by an eager openness, all "having the capacity to reach beyond one's own clan and culture and embrace ever-widening circles by humanity." The kind of community to which Proctor pointed—and that has full scriptural warrant—results from "acknowledging one another's total personhood, looking upon persons as equals to ourselves and not as our pawns or instruments of our design."[3] Preaching can keep such a vision alive in such a world as ours. Preaching can help to bring that vision into reality.

Howard Thurman was also a preaching witness infused with concern to shape community as God desires it. He was always preaching about our need to acknowledge and accept each other, our need to deal totally with one another, explaining that an alliance with God mandates it. And he was right, because the biblical concern for human togetherness is, indeed, "the ethical imperative of religious experience."[4] Every time we preach we should know that the all-embracing love of God is "an established center out of at last we can function

---

3. Samuel D. Proctor, *My Moral Odyssey* (Valley Forge, Pa.: Judson Press, 1989), 149.

4. Howard Thurman, *Disciplines of the Spirit* (New York: Harper & Row, 1963), 121.

and relate" to others.[5] Yes, preaching the counsel of God's love includes voicing God's concern for human togetherness. Preaching is an agency by which that love expresses itself to bring the hearers into community—and preaching is a giant part of the divine strategy for shaping and sustaining that community. This is why Kelly Miller Smith could state the matter so categorically in these words: "Preaching has a unifying function because it assembles the world around the incarnational event and addresses the world's issues through that event."[6]

The passionate interest of Thurman, Proctor, and Smith in the shaping of community through their work involved something more than a love of democracy, and it grew out of something other than a sentimental idealism about the civilizing values of working to become "one nation under God." Howard Thurman, Samuel Proctor, and Kelly Miller Smith were all preachers who took seriously the biblical concern for the togetherness of human life in celebration of God and the furtherance of the divine purpose for our lives. They honored the biblical tradition that God is the source, the ground, and the guide of all life. But there was another tradition from which they all drew: their African American heritage of meanings and understandings about the nature and crucial importance of community. These two traditions linked in their thought and living, and that linkage enriched them for their creative ministries in the United States and beyond.

Howard Thurman, Samuel Proctor, and Kelly Miller Smith, like many others not so prominent, were African Americans who knew the torments of being viewed and treated as outsiders in the land of their birth simply because they were black. Exposed to racism across their years while seeking to relate to the

---

5. Howard Thurman, *The Search for Common Ground: An Inquiry into the Basis of Man's Experience of Community* (New York: Harper & Row, 1971), 104.

6. Kelly Miller Smith, *Social Crisis Preaching,* the Lyman Beecher Lectures 1983 (Macon, Ga.: Mercer University Press, 1984), 19.

majority culture, each man had reasons enough to question the sincerity of the American system of democracy, to get side-tracked in lamenting, or to become prickly or even poisoned in disposition. But each one instead drew steadily upon the strengths and insights of the Christian faith and that influential cultural heritage that helped them to see why a creative response to human friction was a *must*. The result of their personal struggles was a disciplined understanding and use of agape love, and each man preached from a stance of openness, acceptance, and willingness to be in community.

The thought out of which these men preached was fed by their common heritage of spirituality. The moral discourse into which they invited their hearers called upon one and all to understand that they viewed community as "the paramount social reality apart from which humanity cannot exist" and to realize that full participation in the life and support of genuine community "comprises the nature of religious devotion."[7] We who are called and sent to preach are under the necessity to shape community through our work.

The community we seek to shape through preaching usually begins as a crowd, a gathering that is not singular but multiple in cast and mind. It begins as a heterogeneous mass of persons whose common point of togetherness is that they are all at the same place at the same time. Some in the crowd are mere fascinated spectators, but some others are ardent disciples in faith. Some are there as active church members who depend readily upon fellowship with other members for encouragement and nurture, persons who are more oriented to life within the group, while some others are there before the preacher whose bent is toward the world beyond the group. To be sure, there are many concerns that predetermine the personal interest at work

---

7. Peter J. Paris, *The Spirituality of African Peoples: The Search for a Common Moral Discourse* (Minneapolis: Fortress Press, 1995), 51.

in the minds and lives of those who gather where preaching takes place, and those concerns will affect the level and extent of each hearer's interest in the preacher's presence and purpose.

This multiple cast of an audience can make any preacher's feeling of vulnerability an even greater burden, unless he or she is steadied by the realization that something meaningful can happen if the sharing is focused and responsible. *Focused* is the right word, because preaching is done for situated persons, not for the crowds, and every hearing person is to be viewed as a candidate for engagement with God.

The listeners' interest, agreement, and involvement are more readily gained when there is a genuine and vital interest on our part to engage them with God's concern for them and when we never stoop in dishonesty "to affect an interest in our people and a sympathy with them that we do not in reality feel."[8] Willard L. Sperry once commented that "preaching is, for the [one] who does it, a dual transaction which must reckon with Christian truth on the one hand and with the mind of the hearer on the other hand."[9] In actual fact, preaching involves still another transaction, because the hearer is called into a relationship not only with the truth being spoken but with the bearer of that truth as well. It is crucial to preaching, therefore, that our witness be given out of a contagious caring, that we share our very soul in preaching, that we be openly and unabashedly personal as we preach. In this way we can reflect incarnational meanings that can draw our hearers into a circle of mutual acceptance and full regard.

D. Stuart Briscoe has told about an old Texas preacher who complained that when standing before his congregation to preach, the people out before him looked like hooting owls sitting on tombstones—motionless and soundless, as if uncompre-

---

8. Alexander Whyte, *Bunyan's Characters* (Philadelphia: Presbyterian Board of Education and Sabbath-School Work, 1893), 277.

9. Willard L. Sperry, *We Prophesy in Part: A Re-examination of the Liberty of Prophesying* (New York: Harper and Bros., 1938), v.

hending or, at worst, uninterested. Briscoe found himself wondering how that preacher managed to remain in that pulpit. But on further thought it occurred to him that there might well be some connection between the apparent numbness of the people and that preacher's presentation. "Could it be," he wondered, "that they were unmoved because they could not see any relevance in what he had to say?"[10] Relevance is a key factor in preaching, as we all know, but so is a warm and contagious regard for the listeners. Hearers usually respond in relation to the perceived openness and concern projected by the one speaking to them.

In his autobiography, *Unfinished Journey,* violinist Yehudi Menuhin gives some reflections about audience reactions he has observed while performing around the world and across the years. Menuhin commented that while performing in Paris, Rome, Vienna, Berlin, London, and elsewhere, he sometimes has sensed a much-welcomed anticipation within the audience, but that he has sometimes been disappointed by a lack of commitment to the occasion or to what he has chosen to play. Sometimes the audience was disciplined and polite, at other times very open and attentive. Sometimes interested listeners afterward sought him in his dressing room to talk about some interpretation he had given. Alas, there were also those times when he was aware of playing to "unrepentant individualists," as he called them, persons whose surrender he had to win![11] Of his audiences in the United States, Menuhin lauded openness of mind and a national predisposition to favor what is new. But he also said that there is a caution most American listeners exercise against the "regimentation of authority or tradition."[12]

---

10. D. Stuart Briscoe, "Hooting Owls on Tombstones," in *A Passion for Preaching: Reflections on the Art of Preaching, Essays in Honor of Stephen F. Olford,* ed. David L. Olford (Nashville: Thomas Nelson, 1989), 68.

11. Yehudi Menuhin, *Unfinished Journey* (New York: Alfred A. Knopf, 1977), see 270-71.

12. Ibid., 272.

Like musicians, preachers have to deal sometimes with "unrepentant individualists," with those who initially resist authority and tradition. Learning how to deal with such persons is a must, because the strain of it all can aggravate the sense of being under threat; it can heighten one's sense of inwardness. Perceptive listeners can usually discern the preacher's uneasiness when the pressures of apparent resistance are not handled well. This is why the preacher's regard for the listeners—all of them—must be genuine, and that regard must show itself despite what "unrepentant individualists" do to dare to differ with our message and intent.

Jesus often had to deal with unrepentant individualists. The ministry of Jesus was so creative that he caught the public imagination. Crowds followed him. But he was sometimes so controversial that he caught the public rage, and the crowds thinned out. John 6:66-67 documents one such instance. The narrative there shows a once-thronging crowd thinning out because something Jesus said did not please some of his hearers. Jesus watched those persons leave. Some of them had, perhaps, misunderstood him. Some had misgivings about his motives. Some others outrightly disagreed with him. When all movement ceased, Jesus set his eyes upon the waiting remnant still at his side and put this question to them: "Do you also wish to go away?" (John 6:67 NRSV). Jesus wanted those who remained to take him seriously. He was testing their minds and spirits, intent to lead them beyond being merely fascinated so that they would become ardent disciples. He wanted to ready them all for life on God's terms.

In connection with the fact that some who left Jesus on that occasion did so because what he said did not please them, it is important to remind ourselves that as speakers we are under some obligation to move in the direction of our hearers, in some measure to "please" them. We all know that an alert, intent speaker must have an approach in keeping with what the hearers know, how they think, how they feel about things, and how they can best receive what is being said. And we all know that real communication is blocked when a speaker fails to take all of this into account.

James Herman Robinson told how he learned this the hard way, having fumbled his way through a series of six "heavy" sermons during the first three months of ministry in his New York City church. The fourth sermon in his series was titled "The Ontological Argument for the Proof of the Existence of God." (There was even a subtitle: "Discussed from the Point of View of Anselm, Descartes, and Kant"!) Following the service in which he preached that sermon, a wise deaconess invited the young pastor to her home for a meal. After the meal she offered some gently spoken advice. She advised him to slow the pace and lessen the amount of information being offered in his preaching. She sought to assure him that if he would begin with the people where they were, they would rightly follow. "They taught you theology, psychology, and philosophy in the seminary," she advised, "but you haven't learned any 'peopleology.' You've been trying to give us in three weeks what you learned in three years. Next Sunday morning, preach about something that we know something about, and give us just a little something new." The young pastor's pride was further punctured when the wise deaconess smiled and commented, with her face half turned away, "It would be well if you preached on something you know about, too."[13]

We would never charge Jesus with failing to plan well for his preaching. Addressing as he did all sorts of persons, with their varied interests, conditions, and needs, Jesus set himself to communicate aptly. His similes, similitudes, metaphors, and

---

13. James H. Robinson, *Adventurous Preaching,* the Lyman Beecher Lectures 1955 (Great Keck, N.Y.: Channel Press, 1956), esp. 34-35. See also Robinson's autobiography, *Road Without Turning: The Story of Reverend James H. Robinson* (New York: Farrar, Straus and Company, 1950), 230.

parables are immediate proof. From what the existing records of his ministry indicate, Jesus was not formal or speculative when he preached; his speech was rather warm, open, direct, pictorial, dynamic, exciting, and sometimes extravagant, as when he used hyperbole. Jesus preached to be understood. He always sought to carry his hearers along with him, step by step, but he also had to give them something new. Jesus always considered his audience, but his audiences did not always rightly consider him. Both speaker and listeners are under a mutual obligation: They should match each other in openness, purpose, and concern. When they don't match, understanding is blocked, communication is thwarted, and togetherness between speaker and audience fails to happen. That failure to meet sometimes happened in the ministry of Jesus, and it will sometimes happen to us. As servants we are not above our master. But, like our Lord, we must work faithfully at our task, so that we are not the cause for a failed communication when we preach.

Appeal in Preaching

Togetherness between preacher and people is often encouraged by our means of appeal. Specific preparation for the pulpit presupposes a clear objective to be reached by preaching and some appealing means by which that objective is pursued. The framework (structure and sequencing) of the message should have appeal. It should be planned well to elicit interest and to reward that interest through shared insight and guided reflection. A sense of immediacy should be conveyed so that the preaching can rightly lead to the motivated attitudes and action the preacher seeks to inspire.

Appeal in preaching often depends on the right words for what one seeks to share. It is possible to show inadvertent disregard for hearers in the way we word our sermons. This is surely the case when a preacher uses the jargon of the academy in the pulpit, when the words chosen for the message are sensed by the hearers as a restricted or private language. "What makes a language private," Alfred J. Ayer explained, "is simply the fact that it satisfies the purpose of being intelligible only to a single person, or to a restricted set of people."[14] Church jargon, so familar to us, can be problematic in some settings, especially in this day, when the vast populace is known to be unfamiliar with both biblical lore and biblical terms. We who preach must be sensitive to the need to remain faithful to the biblical faith and to voice that witness with such terms and expressions as will make it readily understood in the many new settings where we must do our work.

No sermon can be effective that lacks listener focus, and the way we word our witness can encourage or impede the way a hearer is made to feel about listening. Preaching stands fulfilled only when it has penetrated the listener's consciousness, not when it was but the preacher's self-expression. The listener's interest is essential to communal concern, and proper planning and projection by the preacher, steeped in the spirit of prayer, can be blessed by God to gain that interest, reward that interest, and harness that interest for a life of sustained faith and obedient trust before God. No small part of this whole process has to do with our choice and use of words in preaching.

As preachers we must seek increasingly to understand and to use language with which our listeners can most readily understand, aware of the sentiments and concerns that affect their listening level. Listening is not just a rational action; it is a relational and subjective one. It involves feelings as well as thought. Henry H. Mitchell has aptly and helpfully treated this matter in his seminal book *The Recovery of Preaching*,[15] and so

---

14. Alfred J. Ayer, *The Concept of a Person and Other Essays* (London: Macmillan, 1968), 36.

15. Henry H. Mitchell, *The Recovery of Preaching,* the Lyman Beecher Lectures (San Francisco: Harper & Row, 1974), esp. chaps. 2–3, and 151-58.

has David Buttrick in his pace-setting study of how the language of preaching functions in shaping both a personal consciousness within a listener and a communal consciousness within a congregation.[16] Mitchell has rightly reminded us that effective preaching has usually happened when there has been "the willingness and ability of preachers to sit where their people sit, existentially and culturally," when the preaching is addressed to the person as a whole. Buttrick has advised us anew what ordinary human language can do for our purpose, provided we use it in the service of disclosure.[17] Rightly planned and projected, a sermon can provide an opening for an experience in which both preacher and people can stand exposed to mediated meaning and mediated Presence. It is to such an end that full-scale preaching always seeks to move.

There is still validity, as I see it, in the personal-openness appeal in preaching, by which I mean opening to the hearers' view some pertinent aspect of one's own experience with life and truth. Some preachers do a great deal of this, while others are reticent about doing it at all, fearful lest they be viewed as calling undue attention to themselves. John Calvin was more reticent about voicing his own experience publicly than was Martin Luther; Luther quite often called attention to some personal experience in seeking to illuminate some point or issue while preaching. Calvin felt free to use much "wit and imagery" in the pulpit, trusting the power of words to accomplish his end; while his manner of preaching was lively, passionate, direct, intimate, and clear, he avoided letting himself be seen in his sermons.[18] Luther was known to point out that a text must be heard for what it is saying, but he also called attention to the way

16. David Buttrick, *Homiletic: Moves and Structures* (Philadelphia: Fortress Press, 1987), esp. 196-98, 276-77.

17. See Mitchell, *The Recovery of Preaching*, 11; Buttrick, *Homiletic*, 198.

18. See T. H. L. Parker, *John Calvin: A Biography* (Philadelphia: Westminster Press, 1975), 92.

personal experiences from the preacher's life can often illuminate aspects of meaning in a text.[19]

There is so much to consider in citing personal experience while preaching, but even if one chooses not to do so, the element of appeal need not be missing in one's handling of the truth. Truth can be handled appealingly in more than one way. There are, indeed, myriad ways by which our witness can be aptly handled for those who are present to hear us give it. As Sir Russell Brain once put it, "Indeed, we may come to the conclusion that the important thing about truth is not that it should be naked, but what clothes suit it best, and whether it should not sometimes dress up for special occasions."[20] Pertinent illustrations are such colorful clothes, even if they are not drawn from one's own life experience.

I recall a certain sermon I preached to help my hearers deal with religious prejudice. My concern was to encourage a change in stance among any hearers whose view of the church was so narrow as to involve only those who looked, spoke, and acted like themselves—and were members of the same church group. I knew that to some my counsel for change would seem like a hard saying, so I softened the anticipated criticism with a bit of humor as I drew upon a personal experience. I told of being aboard an airplane with my wife. The preparations for take-off were being made, and the usual announcement by the stewardess seemed to be disregarded by a few of the passengers. One fellow was sitting just ahead and across the aisle from me, so preoccupied (or perhaps overly familiar with such instructions being offered) in his reading that he failed to do what was advised. His tray table was still down in front of him, and a book was propped open on it. I watched him for a bit, wondering if he had heard

---

19. See Jaroslav Pelikan, *Luther the Expositor,* companion vol. to *Luther's Works* (St. Louis: Concordia, 1959), 188.

20. Sir Russell Brain, *The Nature of Experience* (London: Oxford University Press, 1959), 3.

the stewardess. After a bit, I said to my wife, "People just don't listen anymore; they're too preoccupied!" Not long afterward, as the stewardess made her way down the aisle, she saw that he had not prepared himself for take-off, so she stood beside him and courteously touched his shoulder while lifting his open book from the tray table to break his concentration. She even smiled as she raised his tray table and fastened it to the back of the seat in front of him. I overheard her ask him to fasten his seatbelt. I watched it all, somewhat amused, but with a bit of disgust as well. Meanwhile the plane was being backed off the ramp. As I was still reflecting on the other passenger's obtuseness, the stewardess turned in my direction, checking my seatbelt, and as she stood in front of me I shuddered! Looking down, I suddenly realized that I had not fastened my seatbelt! Just as she was about to say something to me, I grabbed the belt ends, hooked them quickly, and looked up at her with a kind of half-guilty smile! In watching the other passenger, I had failed to notice my own lack of listening! The congregation roared with laughter at my confession, but as that laughter ebbed, I said, "This also happens in religious matters." And with that my point was made. The humor helped my counsel to be heard, giving its truthfulness an added appeal. I risked being personal in order to be more pertinent; I had made a confession that laid a claim upon my hearers to undergo a needed change. In speaking to the hearers about my experience, I appealingly prodded them to think more intently about their own attitudes and views. There is a tasteful way to tell about some aspect of one's own life while addressing needs in the lives of others, and there is a lively appeal in the preaching that aptly does so. That appeal also generates togetherness!

The most fundamental means of appeal for togetherness, however, is to provide a common foundation and a common focus for listening. The use of a strategic text of Scripture is both a traditional and a promising way to do so.

In connection with the importance and promise of Scripture for preaching, I recall what the late L. Nelson Bell once wrote about this. A physician-surgeon (and father of Ruth Bell Graham, wife of evangelist Billy Graham), Bell likened much contemporary preaching that lacked a textual base to surgery without using a scalpel. The surgeon, Bell stated, merely made passes over the patient while in the operating room. Afterward, an observing intern would confess his dismay about the procedure, since it left the patient in exactly the same condition. Without a knife's being applied to the problem area, the source of the illness remained untouched. In like manner, Bell asserted, if a person's trip to the worship setting does not expose him or her to the Word of God about life, then no real change is possible in the inward condition. His point remains vividly with me: The preacher without a Scripture text is like a surgeon without a scalpel.[21]

In addition to the use of a text for one's sermon logic, sermon life, and kerygmatic purpose, it also provides the basis for a focus for the congregated hearers. Gerhard Ebeling once explained, "The text is not there for its own sake, but for the sake of the word-event which is the origin and also the future of the text."[22] The directional benefit of the text is a means for togetherness between God and hearers, with the preacher and people sharing together as fellow worshipers. The use of a text serves more than sentiment and honors more than custom; it provides both preacher and people the appealing means for a common focus and the sure foundation to all for a common faith.

---

21. L. Nelson Bell, "Missing—One Knife," *Christianity Today,* August 1970, 34-35 (reprint of October 10, 1960, editorial).

22. Gerhard Ebeling, *Theology and Proclamation,* ed. and trans. John Riches (Philadelphia: Fortress Press, 1966), 28.

Affirming Truth Together

As preachers, we are charged with speaking the Word of the Lord, the sounding forth of which has been referred to by psychologist Paul W. Pruyser as one among the "numinous noises of worship."[23] We are authorized to speak that Word, to utter the sounds that open up spiritual meanings to the hearer. The numinous sounds associated with our reason for service relate our hearers to distinct religious facts and stir the most responsible feelings. Our sounding forth of God's Word through our witness is a time-honored agency by which human perceptions are engaged, evaluated, expanded, and ennobled. And when preaching of that given Word is matched by the people's desire to listen with full openness to it, then the whole experience of worship deepens and character is formed and confirmed.

It is the solemn responsibility of the preacher to see to it that her or his utterings are, indeed, "numinous" sounds, the true sharing of a word from God. A serious preacher will pray for, plan aptly, and deliver nothing less than this. In all honesty, we might have to admit that we have at times done less than this, that by circumstance or default we have done only a meager part of it. Irving Kolodin, a music critic, wrote something about music that helps to explain what I mean by a "meager part of it." Kolodin tells us that his earliest contact with musical instruments was in the family home when he was five years old. He was given a violin, and his older brother was given a piano. Young Irving wished he had been given the piano rather than the violin, however, because of the difference in the amount of sound the piano gave forth. The piano sound seemed so full, so total, so engrossing; he found himself associating full music with the piano sound, while what the violin offered was only a part of

---

23. Paul W. Pruyser, *A Dynamic Psychology of Religion* (New York: Harper & Row, 1968), 21.

music.[24] As regards preaching, perhaps all of us have experienced the ministry of someone whose "numinous noises" in the pulpit made us associate the service as so full, so total, and so engrossing that we thought of our own efforts in handling the given Word as a meager part of what preaching was meant to be. This is a circumstance, a fall-out from that inwardness with which we are so well acquainted. But let it not be the result of default, the sad harvest from neglected study, squandered time, or undisciplined living.

As preachers, our business is to effect an interaction between those who hear us and the Word we are sent to share with them. We do so through sight and sound, our presence and our proclamation. Both are germane to effect the togetherness preaching was appointed to make possible. Our business is more than facilitating a group interaction; it is to lead people to invest themselves in God's grace and involve themselves in God's will. As David H. C. Read voiced it, people "listen to a sermon expecting grace."[25]

C. S. Lewis once called attention to the three elements peculiar to all developed religions, and then reported that Christianity has a fourth element entirely unique to it. The first element is the experience of the numinous, which excites awe in the presence of the deity; the second element is the consciousness of moral law; the third is a sense of personal obligation or accountability. That fourth element, peculiar to the Christian faith—to whose forwarding we have been called—is the impact of the historical event of Jesus Christ upon human life and hope.[26] Our preaching, when true to its origins, heralds such a word. As Emil Brunner has rightly explained, "Where there is

---

24. Irving Kolodin, *In Quest of Music: A Journey in Time* (Garden City, N.Y.: Doubleday, Inc., 1980), ix.

25. David H. C. Read, *Sent from God: The Enduring Power and Mystery of Preaching*, the Lyman Beecher Lectures 1973 (Nashville: Abingdon Press, 1974), 56.

26. C. S. Lewis, *The Problem of Pain* (New York: Macmillan, 1962), 16-24.

true preaching, where, in the obedience of faith to the command of the Lord and in the authority of His Spirit the Word is proclaimed, there, in spite of all appearances to the contrary, the most important thing that ever happens upon this earth takes place."[27]

The preaching moment deepens when worshipers have some freedom to register their affirmation to the preacher's accents. There are those times in worship when the spirit of the occasion blesses all persons who are fully open to it, and the very excitement stirred by the mediated meaning, together with a sense of awe, almost demands some expressiveness on the part of the people, as in the openly spoken "Amen!" and "Preach it!" of the African American tradition. While this form of verbal response might not commend itself to every cultural setting, it is illustrative of the kind of togetherness preaching can encourage. As for the black church setting, the verbal "Amen" from the worshipers is usually to affirm the preacher's witness; it is periodic, intermittent, sometimes vociferously uttered—and encouraged by some preachers who feel less inhibited because of this audience witness. But such audible responses are not the only immediate indicators of dialogue togetherness. Henry H. Mitchell has rightly explained that "smiles and other facial expressions, nodding of the head, intensity of gaze, and edge-of-the-seat position all contribute to the communication between preacher and people."[28]

Dietrich Bonhoeffer was deeply moved by the free expressions of togetherness between preacher and people while visiting Abyssinian Baptist Church, in New York, during his stay in America (1930–31). Albert Franklin Fisher, a black seminarian at Union Theological Seminary, where they both were studying, had befriended the young German scholar and wanted to expose

---

27. Emil Brunner, *Revelation and Reason*, ed. and trans. Olive Wyon (Philadelphia: Westminster Press, 1946), 142.

28. Mitchell, *The Recovery of Preaching*, 117.

him to the rich and creative worship of that black spiritual community as Bonhoeffer spent time visiting among the many churches of the city.[29] Doing his field work at Abyssinian Church at the time, Fisher asked Bonhoeffer to work along with him there during the spring term of 1931, and together they taught a Sunday school class for boys.[30] That weekly service role gave Bonhoeffer insight into many aspects of that church's life, especially how its programming related faith and work, piety and social outreach. Bonhoeffer also *felt* the delights of being in a setting where the Word was uttered in freedom and where the worshipers freely registered their acceptance of and regard for that Word. Years later, back in Germany, Bonhoeffer confessed what that time in the black church setting had meant to his life and thought. But even before leaving the United States after that brief stay, Bonhoeffer told some of his German-speaking friends at Union Seminary what joy had been his to hear and see black believers responding so openly with verbal responses to his preaching.[31] Bonhoeffer was impressed by the spirit of the occasion and the open tokens of togetherness the preaching encouraged.

Bonhoeffer's experience of worship among black churches during his visit to the United States left a deep imprint in his

---

29. See Eberhard Bethge, *Dietrich Bonhoeffer: Man of Vision, Man of Courage*, trans. Eric Mosbacher et al., ed. Edwin Robertson (New York: Harper & Row, 1970), esp. 109-10, 113-14, 138. For Bonhoeffer's impressions while involved in these experiences, see Dietrich Bonhoeffer, *No Rusty Swords: Letters, Lectures and Notes 1928–1936*, ed. Edwin H. Robertson (New York: Harper & Row, 1965), esp. 112-14. See also personal accounts about Bonhoeffer's life during this period in Paul Lehmann's "Paradox of Discipleship," in *I Knew Dietrich Bonhoeffer*, ed. Wolf-Dieter Zimmerman and Ronald Gregor Smith, trans. Kathe Gregor Smith (New York: Harper & Row, 1966), esp. 41-45.

30. Adam Clayton Powell, Sr., *Against the Tide: An Autobiography* (New York: Richard R. Smith, 1938), 190, made reference to "a German teacher in the Sunday school." Bethge's biography identifies that German as Dietrich Bonhoeffer.

31. See Ruth Zerner, "Dietrich Bonhoeffer's American Experiences: People, Letters, and Papers from Union Seminary," *Union Seminary Quarterly Review* XXXI/4 (Summer 1976): esp. 269-70.

spirit. In later years, in Germany, he sometimes played his records of black Spirituals for the students studying under him at Finkenwalde, and he would talk excitedly to them about piety, theology, and worship as he had known these among the African Americans.[32] Bonhoeffer's own preaching style became more direct after his worship times among black congregations, and he gave increased attention to the community theme that had earlier claimed his thought.

Interestingly, although Bonhoeffer never regularly attended morning chapel at Union during his stay there—and he even lamented the sad state of worship among some of the New York churches he had visited—he went weekly, and with passionate interest, to the Abyssinian Baptist Church.[33] Perhaps the best explanation for his actions is found in this assessment he wrote of what he was experiencing there: "One may also say that nowhere is revival preaching still so vigorous and so widespread as among the Negroes, that here the Gospel of Jesus Christ, the saviour of the sinner, is really preached and accepted with great welcome and visible emotion."[34]

At Abyssinian Church, Bonhoeffer had been part of a congregational worship setting in which togetherness prevailed between preacher Adam Clayton Powell, Sr., and the avid hearers of his "numinous noises."[35] There he experienced involvement in a life-flow where utterance and openness were contagious. So he was reminiscing out of more than his Lutheran heritage when he later commented that "a truly evangelical sermon must be like offering a child a fine red apple or offering a thirsty man a cool glass of water and saying: "Wouldn't

---

32. See Lehmann, "Years in Berlin," *I Knew Dietrich Bonhoeffer,* 64-65.
33. See Bethge, *Dietrich Bonhoeffer,* 116.
34. Bonhoeffer, *No Rusty Swords,* 113.
35. On the preaching of Adam Clayton Powell, Sr., see Adam Clayton Powell, Jr., *Adam by Adam: The Autobiography of Adam Clayton Powell, Jr.* (New York: The Dial Press, 1971), esp. 7-10, 49-50.

you like it.' "[36] For Bonhoeffer, many experiences of realized togetherness and meaning in worship stood behind his statement to Franz Hildebrandt: "Every sermon must be an event."[37]

Helmut Thielicke, another German theologian, also confessed how moved he had been by the eventful worship he experienced as guest preacher in a black church in Chicago in 1962, during his second visit to the United States. As the responsive congregation entered into dialogue with his preaching, Thielicke became so uplifted and free that the experience registered itself as one of the most impressive in his years of pulpit ministry. Here is what he recorded about that unforgettable event in his autobiography:

> With regard to the worship services that I held in Chicago, I was especially impressed with a sermon that I gave in a Negro congregation. At first there were worries about my sermon there because people were concerned that the congregation would not understand me. However, they responded enthusiastically and interrupted my sermon continually with loud exclamations like: "Yes, Lord!," "Hallelujah," "Amen!" and many other exclamations. So that in turn inspired me in a way that *I felt like I was taken by a huge wave and almost experienced what is known in the English language as the story of Pentecost, and I became a willing instrument.*[38]

The sharing that took place between Thielicke and the congregants helped to shape the climate for that eventfulness. It is to a discussion of the preacher's part in getting ready for this eventfulness that we now turn.

---

36. Bethge, *Dietrich Bonhoeffer,* 175.
37. Ibid.
38. Helmut Thielicke, *Zu Gast auf einem Schonen Stern* (Hamburg: Hoffman, und Campe Verlag, 1984), 462, italics added. I am indebted to Dr. Robert Smith, Jr., professor of preaching at Southern Baptist Theological Seminary, and my former student, for calling to my attention this experience of Thielicke. Smith prepared this translation from the German publication, and I use it here with his permission.

CHAPTER FOUR

The Eventfulness
of Preaching

In his book *The Hero in History,* philosopher Sidney Hook has given us a section that offers his insights about what he has termed the "eventful" person. I have included a portion of that section to help us consider our work and possibilities as preachers:

> The *eventful* [person] in history is any [person] whose actions influenced subsequent developments along a quite different course than would have been followed if their actions had not been taken. The event-making [person] is an eventful [person] whose actions are the consequences of outstanding capabilities of intelligence, will, and character rather than of accidents of position.[1]

I paused long in thought after first encountering those words, because I was stirred by their implication regarding our work as preachers. Is not the purpose of preaching to influence lives to take directions that would not have been possible to take otherwise? Is not the preacher sent to be an event maker? Even if Hook's comment about "outstanding capacities of intelligence" does not apply to very many of us—since the apostle's assess-

---

1. Sidney Hook, *The Hero in History* (New York: John Day Co., 1943), 154.

ment reminds us that "not many of [us] were wise by human standards; not many were influential; not many were of noble birth" (1 Cor. 1:26)—are we not enjoined by God to be persons of will and character, faithful servants whose influence depends on something other than mere position? How can we meet these demands and experience these possibilities?

Acknowledging Our Limits and Needs

I will be the first to admit that there are times when we who preach do not feel like event-making persons. There is, for one thing, our feelings as we live with the perennial problem of the "foolishness of our proclamation" as Paul termed it (1 Cor. 1:21). The context and content of preaching are always under the judgmental scrutiny of the "wise" and learned in every age and generation. The kerygma has never been humanly assessed as reasonable, and what the Christian faith holds up as being of eternal importance has never met the human test of philosophical logic, the intellectual standards of the academy, or reasonings about common pragmatic purpose. Preaching is perennially under question by those whose lives and concerns are steadily influenced by what is measurable. Tightly geared to computer tapes, data processing, electronic gadgetry, the Internet, and entertainment, ours is an involvement-participatory oriented society whose members do not wish to listen to serious preaching but to be entertained and have their emotions engaged. If preaching does not do this for them, then it is seen as an activity that promises too little, and, therefore, is a time-wasting problem to be avoided.

Consider also our feelings as we wrestle with the problem of what Joseph Sittler called the minister's "macerated life."[2] How can one preach with inner security and prophetic focus when so

2. Joseph Sittler, *The Ecology of Faith* (Philadelphia: Muhlenburg Press, 1961), esp. 76-88.

many priorities steadily compete for time and attention, when so many urgencies fill and order our days? The demands on our time and attention never cease, and our need for morale is insistent, not to mention the imperative for mature responses on our part to the pressures of our work.

Who feels like an event maker as we reel under the impact of the knowledge explosion in our time? The passing of each day uncovers more and more about which we are ignorant or, at best, ill informed. All of this affects us—and severely. Who has not been guilty of daring to speak boldly and eagerly about matters whose true substance we did not fully know or adequately understand? We are not sent to preach the new directions in science, but whose ruminations in sermon preparation have not been clarified by using the scientific method in the quest to explore and understand so that we can declare and explain? There is so much that we do not know—understandably—because, as the physicists long told us, the *nature* of reality is far more complex than the *picture* of reality. It is still for us as Paul acknowledged about himself: Being human, we are always in the state of knowing "in part" (1 Cor. 13:12*b*); we are always eager and seeking to know more. The impact of the knowledge explosion keeps us feeling far behind in our store of information, but we are in serious trouble if we feel so uncertain that we cannot use the Bible with trust or voice the gospel message with the conviction and freedom its purpose makes necessary. Competing religious notions and even non-religious interpretations of life are multiplying around us, meeting us at every turn we make. Given our pluralistic society, who, indeed, feels sufficient to the task?

There are still other problems that press upon us, making us feel uneventful. There is the problem that so many of the people we seek to serve are uninformed or ill-informed church members, whose consumer-oriented view of the church and spiritual matters crowds us in ways that threaten our training, the church tradition we hold as valuable, and our God-given assignment to be ministers of the Word to them. Secularity, group projects, and the encroachments of civil religion have taken their toll upon church people, while inadequate views about eschatological matters undercut the spirit of evangelism. Preaching is in trouble when there is no inspirational climate among church members to hear the gospel restated and its implications explored for nurture and guidance.

There is yet another problem we face in seeking to be event-making persons. There is a changed expectation among so many about what preaching is or should do. There is a story from the early 1920s about a conversation that took place between a famous concert pianist and a noted United States senator during a dinner party. The senator had been sitting beside the musician for awhile, saying nothing as they ate, when he finally felt compelled to say something out of mere politeness. Aware that Enrico Caruso, the great tenor, had recently died, the senator cleared his throat and ventured a question about the concert world. "Do you think that music will continue," he innocently inquired, "now that Caruso is dead?"[3] The senator meant well, but he was like so many others during that period who knew absolutely nothing else about music except the name Caruso, whose records helped to make the phonograph a household item. The voice of Caruso established a style that dominated the singing craft of his day. His musicality, magnetism, dramatic freedom, and elegance were pacesetting. When he died, music received a heavy blow, in many minds. Caruso died, but music lives on.

I have cited that story because many in our day have raised that uninformed senator's lament with reference to preaching. Their brand of preacher having passed from this life, they speak

3. See George Movshon, "Enrico Caruso, Father of Us All," *High Fidelity* (September 1969): 77.

as if preaching itself has died, that the future of preaching went to the grave with the preacher they favored. We must readily admit, and not lament, that there have been those preachers whose style, freedom, bearing, and themes set standards against which we are being measured. One of the questions that I am constantly asked in my travels is, "Who are the great preachers today?" Whenever I hear the question, I am mindful again that preaching remains in trouble.

Given the world in which we live, and the many interests that compete in it, preaching has always been in trouble—and it always will be. This only highlights our need to be event makers through our preaching. Although we often feel severely limited as we wrestle with the inward side of our work, and as we look realistically at *words,* the tools of our work, it is important to realize that even our Lord had to do his work with the same tools. Philip Wheelwright once remarked that "the majority of human utterances are thin pipings, as though (Nietzsche remarked) the *Eroica* Symphony were to be scored for two flutes."[4] Yes, how uneventful we feel when, despite all of our best efforts, we watch in weakness and worry as our

Words strain,
Crack and sometimes break, under the burden
Under the tension, slip, slide, perish,
Decay with imprecision, will not stay in place,
Will not stay still.[5]

It must have been out of feeling as we do that Paul wrote, "For since, in the wisdom of God, the world did not know God through wisdom, God decided, through the foolishness of our proclamation, to save those who believe" (1 Cor. 1:21 NRSV).

---

4. Philip Wheelwright, *The Burning Fountain: A Study in the Language of Symbolism* (Bloomington: Indiana University Press, 1954), 3.
5. T. S. Eliot, from "Burnt Norton," in *Collected Poems: 1909–1950* (New York: Harcourt, Brace, Jovanovich, 1971), 21.

Paul's trust in God's wisdom gave him strength for preaching. That trust was his thrust to be an eventful preacher.

There is a kind of folly associated with the preaching task, and this has to do with both the message and the methods employed in voicing it. As for preaching as a method, I have gained increased insight into our situationed work through comparing the setting with that of the stand-up comedian. Here is how Elliot W. Eisner described the comedian's setting:

> He too is before a group in a state of flux. He too provides and responds to a flow of qualities, qualities that cannot always be predicted. To survive on stage the comedian must be able to understand, in qualitative terms, the meaning of the qualities displayed by his audience. When to speed up the pace, when to slow it down, how much time to allow to elapse before the punchline; these decisions are not deduced from a psychological theory of behavior but rather from a highly developed and refined qualitative intelligence that allows qualities to be experienced in the first place, and a repertoire of qualitatively loaded actions from which the comedian can draw.[6]

The paragraph is quite packed, but consider again the correspondences in it to the preacher's setting as we face a listening people: We who preach must seek to capture the movement of minds and spirits within the group; we must seek to harness their interest and direct the state of affairs. We must do this through readiness with words, all of them "qualitatively loaded," and we must have a strict sense of timing, knowing "when to speed up the pace, when to slow it down." All this demands on our part an awareness of what is happening in the group, through a "qualitative intelligence that allows [this] to be experienced in the first place."

Stand-up comedians know that eventfulness must occur and

---

6. Elliott W. Eisner, "The Intelligence of Feeling," in *Facts and Feelings in the Classroom*, ed. Louis J. Rubin (New York: Walker and Co., 1973), 203-4.

that the experienced event is assisted by what is done up front. Everything done is calculated to lead one and all to a climax of impression and reaction. Thus the speech is zestful, the lines are mind-engaging, the imagination is directed, the feelings are tapped. Eventful preaching also depends on certain distinct, up-front elements.

Despite the limitations of human speech, the words we use do have affective aspects. There is strict promise of eventfulness when we have considered the biblical witness, contemplated the audience needs, and developed a "right" approach in relating these in our preaching. There is something of great effect when we have so penetrated the meaning of the text that we can restate its message with such involvement that we seem to be its original source, as it were. When we work systematically with the truth and plan our voicing of it with our hearers in heart as well as in mind—truly intent to help them *see* and *experience* the meaning of what we preach—then we can anticipate and work for a climax of impression out of which the hearers can rightly decide and responsibly act.

On Being Grasped by the Word

An intelligent and practical grasp of the biblical message is imperative for this eventfulness. That right grasp of what we are to say is crucial to pulpit preparation, and it depends on our taking time with the Word and paying strict attention to what that Word reports and means. The very nature and purpose of our call demand that we preach the Word God has sent; but we must know that Word well in order to match the needed message to the right people—and at the right time.

Conductor George Szell was notorious for his attention to detail in preparing to direct from a composer's musical score. Eager to have his music making produce the vision intended in the score, Szell was intolerant of any deviation from the score and its markings. Someone once jokingly said to him that he acted as if the interpretation of even the shortest musical phrase was a matter of life or death. Szell quite seriously replied, "But don't you see, it is. It *is*."[7] Mere pedantry aside, George Szell knew that the full power of music is released only when those who interpret it order themselves by its demands, when they let the music itself remain in control.

Eventful preaching demands an interpreter who is ordered and controlled by the living message in the text. We are sent to share something more than a mere stream of words, however interesting, entertaining, or sensational they might be. We are sent to speak for God and to do so with pointed application for a particular time and people. When the hearers are wise, they will settle for nothing less than an experienced event through preached truth. Eric Sevareid, twenty-six at the time, confessed to Edward R. Murrow that he felt too nervous and lacking in voice to go before the microphone on the television set. Murrow told him not to worry about his voice; he further advised young Sevareid that the media leaders "didn't expect anything sensational, just the truth."[8] And that must be the primary concern of the preacher in determining what to preach.

In applying some truths with clarity, we will need proper illustrative materials. George Johnstone Jeffrey tells of being pulled aside one day by a very busy Glasgow merchant who advised him that the tensions and overbusyness of the working day so tired his brain that the preacher's abstract reasoning in his sermons was sometimes hard to follow for long. The man asked his pastor not to "be above [giving] a simple, child-like story, now and then."[9] Illustrations do help application of truth

---

7. Cited by Gary Graffman, *I Really Should Be Practicing* (Garden City, N.Y.: Doubleday, 1981), 128.

8. Edward R. Murrow, *Newsweek,* November 28, 1977, 130.

9. George Johnstone Jeffrey, *This Grace Wherein We Stand,* Warrack Lectures, 1948 (London: Hodder & Stoughton, 1949), 46.

when we preach. Illustrations make truth vivid, and they make the hearers feel involved. A well-ordered illustration helps to guarantee that the hearers will not be left baffled, overburdened by abstractions, or unmoved.

The Commitment to Preach

The event-making preacher will be more than an observant servant of the Word; he or she will also evince a personal sense of commitment to preaching. The pulpit experience must involve head and heart, thought and emotion, the whole self, if it is to become eventful for an assembled people. It is still as Henry Ward Beecher stated the case long ago: "All true preaching bears the impress of the nature of the preacher, the glow and calm intensity which are derived from his own soul."[10]

The concern for eventfulness will demand more than mere information in preaching. Eventfulness happens through felt insights, through a shared contagion that was evident first in the preaching person. Preaching should not lack tone, personal involvement, or feeling. Only thus can it mediate a sense of God's presence with clear meaning. The meaning should lead the hearer to a clear vision and an involving realization of the need to respond. There is an enormous difference between the mere sharing of facts and the great benefits that follow from an elicited faith. The substance of true preaching involves something more than just passing on information; it includes a certain atmosphere associated with the presence of God.

We all have heard messages that lacked focus, and we are, perhaps, remembering that we ourselves have preached a few. We have heard messages that exhibited no feeling tone, as if the privilege to speak was but casually honored. The moment of preaching is a special time before God; the occasion of hearing

---

10. Henry Ward Beecher, *Yale Lectures on Preaching,* 1st, 2nd, and 3rd series (Boston: Pilgrim Press, 1874), 4.

the Word is a *kairos* time, a time when a divine breakthrough is expected in the listener's life. Those who sense this deeply cannot help responding to it with grateful enthusiasm—not the enthusiasm of overstimulated and undisciplined feelings, but the overflow of gratitude at being gripped by the grace that saves.

An intimate relationship with the text to be used can inspire such enthusiasm for preaching. That intimacy can generate a contagious confidence for an open handling of the text. It is comforting and reassuring to have penetrated the letter of the text and reached its spirit, to have completed the hermeneutical process and to understand the textual purpose. The homiletical task is usually easier when one has done the "first things first," letting the message, the mood, and the structure of the text dictate the focus and outline for the sermon based on it. The deeply appreciated meaning in a text can, indeed, lead to an inspired response for preaching.

So can that deep concern for the welfare of our hearers. Wise preachers know that specific questions of need can call forth the best in us, and because this is true, they will give strict attention to discerning those needs and planning for dealing with them in pulpit work. Those needs are multiple, but in a thumbnail fashion I mention a few:

1. There is the need for answers to questions that press upon the hearer's mind.
2. There is the need to give scriptural guidance on how to live in a godly manner in such a world.
3. There is the need to share truths that grant access to rich understandings about our potential in the will of God.
4. There is the need to promote change, to confront falsity and wrong, to take a stand.

Preaching can do so much to enhance life. It can summon persons to a duty, warn about false paths, encourage a right action, gain supporters to a right cause, and press for a decision about choosing life over death.

In his book *Social Crisis Preaching,* his posthumously published Beecher Lectures at Yale in 1983, Kelly Miller Smith artfully explained that preachers have been and can be eventful figures through preaching. Pointing specifically to social crises and the need for a proper perspective to deal wisely with them, Smith underscored the vital role of preaching as a change-agent, a creative response to crisis, a way of strengthening people to bear the burden of change—or rightly work for change to occur. Recognizing that crisis "comes not only when normal change occurs but also when there is effort to effect change and when there is glaring unmet need." He asserted that Christian faith has a relevant word in times of crisis.[11] He concluded, "The words 'social crisis' and 'preaching' do belong together. As a matter of fact, the term 'preaching' in its most profound meaning includes a concern with social crisis."[12]

Let it be said: Eventful preaching is preaching that is called forth by perceived needs and is informed by scriptural guidance. When done with concern and wise planning, such utterances can, indeed, engage attention and stimulate an event.

I referred earlier to the apparent weakness of our words, to Wheelwright's description of our words as "thin pipings." Let me encourage us all with the reminder that the language of faith involves words that unlock needed meaning and can mediate divine promises. Listen again to some of them: *grace, mercy, hope, deliverance, love, forgiveness, eternal life, peace, heaven*—and the list is redemptively long. Such words are vital signals of God's loving interest in our lives and plan for our possibilities. A strong passion should stir us when we speak these terms. The purpose to which we have been summoned is

---

11. Kelley Miller Smith, *Social Crisis Preaching* (Macon, Ga.: Mercer University Press, 1984), 5.

12. Ibid., 11.

unashamedly soteriological and pastoral. The passion that fires preaching is unmistakably event prone. Under the anointing presence of the Spirit of God, our preaching can grant the needed vision to which our words but feebly point. And such is the miracle of preaching. John R. Claypool was speaking about this result when he confessed: "It is my deepest conviction that when one stands to engage in this particular act, far more takes place than the mere speaking and hearing of words." He added, "Thus it can rightly be called an event, something happens so wholistically that it leaves the kind of impact on one that accompanies participation in any sort of decisive happening."[13]

Preachers as Event Makers

We must prepare ourselves to be eventful preachers. We best do so by cultivating patient togetherness with people, by earnest prayer that keeps us oriented to God, and by the diligent application of ourselves in careful study of God's Word. When our lives are stirred by love, flavored by prayer, and saturated with the informing and revealing Word, we can excite the concern of people when they gather to hear it. That excitement can be at a high level of expectancy when the text is read. Brought together at a textual base that gives both preacher and people a common focus and the foundation for a common faith, both preacher and people find promise for a life-changing, life-enhancing event. It is to such an end that our hermeneutical endeavor must be addressed and our homiletical interest and skills must be subservient.

This accent on the use of biblical texts in preaching does not need to be defended, but it does need to be explained. The concern behind this emphasis is not rooted in an unthinking regard for church tradition; rather, it has to do with an awareness

---

13. John R. Claypool, *The Preaching Event* (Waco: Word Books, 1980), 28.

of how strategic biblical texts serve as distinct truths. Bernard Ramm once put it this way:

> Jesus Christ is the Truth, but we can know him only through the instrumentality of *truths*. Jesus Christ is the living Lord, but we know of this lordship only in the *written* documents of the New Testament. Jesus Christ is Eternal Life, but we know of this eternal life only in the witnessing pages of the New Testament. Only in special revelation do we know that there is a Truth, that there is a Lord, that there is an Eternal life.[14]

The Bible has a reporting, instrumental character; its content serves an end. The church has rightly insisted and expected that its ministers know and preach from Scripture texts. We are brokers of biblical truths, using the texts of the Bible to make known truths that matter supremely, truths that have to do with personal needs and public affairs, truths that lead hearers beyond religion in the past tense to a vital present-tense experience in grace and a vibrant hope that includes more than what is here-and-now. David Buttrick was right to remind us that preaching is "a theological endeavor that seeks to make sense of life now in view of God's graciousness in Jesus Christ."[15] The use of biblical texts is the wisest and safest way to engage in that endeavor.

About a century ago, Henry Van Dyke, a noted preacher who was also a successful man of letters, assessed his times as an age of doubt. I call attention to that assesment because it aptly describes our times, another age of doubt, greatly in need of the benefits of divine truth shared by persons who care about shaping the times. "In calling the present 'an age of doubt,' " Van Dyke commented, "I do not mean that it is the only age in

---

14. Bernard Ramm, *Special Revelation and the Word of God: An Essay on the Contemporary Problem of Revelation* (Grand Rapids: Eerdmans, 1960), 117.

15. David Buttrick, *A Captive Voice: The Liberation of Preaching* (Louisville: Westminster/John Knox Press, 1994), 11.

which doubt has been prevalent, nor that doubt is the only characteristic of the age. I mean simply that it is one of those periods of human history in which the sudden expansion of knowledge and the breaking-up of ancient moulds of thought have produced a profound and widespread feeling of uncertainty in regard to the subject of religion."[16] Does not this same assessment fit our times?

Ours, similarly, is an age of doubt. But in our time the doubt is far more widespread and its effects much more marked. In our time, the questioning temper sustains a persistent tendency to question and to theorize that all too seldom leads to any sure end. The emphasis in our time is on exploring in quest of truth, with no agreed norms to guide the search or help to identify the truth being sought. This age of doubt needs to be addressed by preachers who care about the times, who have a distinct message about the God of truth and the divine provision for a life of meaning; a message that rings loud and clear within our own minds and lives; a message that invites scrutiny, prods thought, stirs a reaction; a message that we must share not only because of a calling to do so but because of a settled confidence about its meaning and importance.

Event making demands that distinct truths be preached. Our pulpit work, rightly understood, is to help persons to experience the grace of God. The climate of our age does not assist us in this quest, since, to quote Ellen T. Charry, "the general populace [is] more familiar with secularism or modern expressions of paganism than with Christianity."[17]

As I see it, the scene we confront in preaching today is like what the apostolic company confronted while preaching throughout the Gentile world of the first century. Interestingly,

---

16. Henry Van Dyke, *The Gospel for an Age of Doubt* (New York: Macmillan, 1896), xvii.
17. Ellen T. Charry, "Academic Theology in Pastoral Perspective," *Theology Today* 1/1 (April 1993): 90.

the apostolic message prevailed. Their story reminds us about the power of heralded truth. The truths those early leaders voiced are still our property, and those truths remain worthy of our trust and proclamation.

Now just as when the church began, the mandated agenda for preaching is to proclaim and interpret for each generation the gracious deed of God in Christ Jesus. It is no small matter to help bring persons to faith, to assist in shaping them as believers, to remain in travail for them, as Paul reports he did (Gal. 4:19), until Christ be formed in them. The work of preaching was commissioned to this end, and this purpose of the gospel steadily reminds those of us who preach to keep this motivation central in our concern. In a day when there seems to be few places on earth for truth to make its way unimpeded, let those of us who preach give truth a broad and ready place of activity within us. Only thus can our pulpit work be what it was intended to be. There are truths to be preached, but the fullest impact from hearing truth preached takes place when our practice stands allied with our speaking. Søren Kierkegaard was pointing to this need in his statement, "The truth is a snare: you cannot have it without being caught. You cannot have the truth in such a way that you catch it, but only in such a way that it catches you."[18]

There are those in our time who have difficulty listening to preachers with a serious openness and trust. Many are those who question whether there are any ministers left worthy of trust. Where preachers are concerned, suspicion fills many minds— suspicions fed by known cases of failure and by a steady spate of media images of ministers as sneaky schemers, hypocritical money grabbers, sex-hungry opportunists, and anxious status seekers. How different the present times are from those days

---

18. Søren Kierkegaard, *The Last Years,* ed. and trans. Ronald G. Smith (New York: Harper & Row, 1965), 133.

when ministers were viewed and known as distinguished, service-minded, truly caring persons!

In his book *No Place for Truth,* theologian David F. Wells gave us his views about the predicament ministers face in the modern world. He isolated the factors he believes produced that predicament and the effects of that predicament on the spirit and the functioning of the churches we serve. Wells suggested that many ministers feel homeless, insecure, and impermanent because they have no honored place in a secularized society or in the church; because they are purveyors of belief, both the world and the church have shunted preachers to the margins of importance. With both church and world hardly interested in what Scripture reports and commends, he further suggested, many ministers find themselves in search of a niche.

The sense of being dislodged from both the church and society has fed our need for a sense of security and status. Wells further asserted that this has led preachers to seek importance and validation such as physicians, lawyers, and others know as "professionals." Wells, a professor of historical and systematic theology, notes that this search for acceptance and validation might well be one of the reasons for the increased popularity of the Doctor of Ministry (D.Min.) degree. Instead of being ordered by a sense of standing before God as a called servant and a pastoral concern to make God's truth known, Wells argues, many ministers have become anxious about their standing in society and thus have professionalized their ministry, aided and abetted by seminary programs that are not centered in the Word of God but in career building. Thus his lament: "The older role of the pastor as broker of truth has been eclipsed by the newer managerial functions."[19] Wells has given us much to discuss and critique, but few would disagree with his judgment that career-

---

19. David Wells, *No Place for Truth* (Grand Rapids: Eerdmans, 1993), 233.

ism in ministry is a capitulation to the spirit of the times, that it dulls our sense of being heralds of truth.

There are truths to be preached. There is truth in Scripture about our common humanity, about our common origin. And that truth is in tandem with the truth from our common experience about our everyday needs. There is a truth to be preached that speaks forthrightly about false norms and idolatrous choices. There is a truth to be proclaimed in the face of marginalizing politics, prejudicial systems, and hegemonic denominationalism. Paul's eagerness to "commend the truth" led him to promote the grace of God in Jesus Christ and to promote that active goodness that works always to overcome evil (see Rom. 12:21).

Truth is a word that was used constantly in the preaching vocabulary of the first-century church. Jesus, who founded the church, was remembered as being "full of grace and truth" (John 1:14). Jesus talked much about truth and promised that those who received his truth would experience true freedom (John 8:32). Jesus referred to the Holy Spirit as the "spirit of truth" (John 14:17; 16:13), and he explained that a part of the Spirit's ministry is to "guide you into all truth" (John 16:13). Interestingly, in one of the few recorded references Jesus made concerning his birth, he told Pilate: "For this reason I was born, and for this I came into the world, to testify to the truth" (John 18:37c).

Paul and other New Testament writers echoed that same honored tradition and concern to testify to the truth. By the time one reaches the Pastoral Letters, there is no doubt about what the first Christian preachers understood and sought to convey when they used the word *truth*. In 1 Timothy, the young pastoral leader was reminded that the church within which God had placed him to serve should be honored always as "the household of God" and as "the pillar and foundation of the truth" (1 Tim. 3:15). The apostolic emphasis on the truth was set over against the problem of false teaching and erroneous thought systems. In all Scripture, truth and error are antithetical. In Scripture, error leads to sad and sorry ends, while truth leads to righteouness, peace, and true fulfillment. Truth refutes error and unmasks deception. Scripture is never unclear or ambiguous about what is truth and what is error, about what is certain and trustworthy in contrast to what is not. This is why we must preach from Scripture texts: They alone help us to know what is genuine and what is not, what is real and what is false, what helps life and what hinders it, what blesses us and what blights us. The truth we are commissioned and expected by God to preach and preserve is an illuminating and distinguishing truth. As truth, it can stand up under any and all scrutiny, and we need have no fear of being put to shame from having stood by it.

We become event makers when our concern in ministering is something deeper and purer than a desire for personal advancement, popularity, and crowd approval. We can check and assess the depth and direction of our concern by asking ourselves in private what it is that gives us the greatest joy as we do our pulpit work. Does my highest moment of delight come when I have been illumined through meticulous study of the Scriptures? Or is my prized moment of joy experienced as I complete a new sermon? Is my chief delight found only as I face the people, addressing them? Or do I feel the highest joy when some hearer reports a decision made because of what I shared in preaching? What gives you the greatest joy as a preacher? Preaching is one of the most important of all human engagements. That engagement should be eventful, not fruitless, bland, or self-indulgent. Such an intimate sharing must not be thwarted by lack of preparation or lack of anticipation. Understood biblically, preaching is not a performance: It is a proclamation with concern for the hearer, a God-directed sharing in which conviction, openness, sincerity, and a divine "mustness" actuate the preacher.

The constraint that leads to eventful preaching is like a deeply felt, energizing song—it possesses the preacher, with a resonating urgency, before it releases itself in overflowing sound. It is a contagion stirred by meaning, and the whole self feels involved in it. Writer Ralph Ellison, musician turned novelist, speaks through one of the characters in his novel *Invisible Man,* saying, "When I have music, I want to *feel* its vibration, not only with my ear but with my whole body."[20] Music was eventful for him; it made things happen in and through him. As one who trained for awhile for the concert world, I understand this. In fact, a major principle in eventful music making is to "carry it in [your] mind, keep it in [your] heart, and hear it with [your] mind's ear,"[21] releasing that music only after it has lived inside the self long enough for the needed expression to mature and come forth, speaking its own witness. This only is "soul music."

Eventful preaching is like that. It is a readied concern to share the truth, and that concern will have lived within the preacher long enough to produce a vision whose vibrations have affected the preacher's whole being. Preaching the given Word *is,* indeed, like handling and being managed by a deeply felt song—since personal involvement is demanded, with intellect and instincts completely engaged in the service of meanings being shared to encourage and effect an experience with God.

Peter's Pentecost day sermon is a clear instance of such eventful preaching. Peter's preaching that day had drive, unction, timeliness, zest, readiness, and relevance. That sermon reached the hearers at the deepest levels of hearing. It was preaching that caused a *happening,* with three thousand people responding decisively in agreement with the preacher's directions. Even now, despite the brevity of Luke's summarized version of it, one can sense in the reported sermon some of the

---

20. Ralph Ellison, *Invisible Man* (New York: Signet Books, 1952), 11.

21. The bracketed pronouns replace the original pronoun "his" in this advisement by Heinrich Neuhaus, noted Russian teacher of pianists. See his *The Art of Piano Playing,* trans. K. A. Leibovitch (New York: Praeger, 1973), 1.

audacious zeal and persuasive thrust that must have been part of the apostle's preaching style. Consider the secure readiness with which he stood and interpreted the Pentecost portent: "These [witnesses] are not drunk, as you suppose. . . . No, this is what was spoken by the prophet Joel" (Acts 2:15-16). He thus spoke to counter a wrong view being voiced by certain critics and to describe aright that experience of such high meaning. Peter saw a need and met it; he crushed a jeering jibe and claimed the hearers in a strategic moment of potent sharing of God's truth about Jesus and their need of him.

It is instructive to observe how Peter lifted Christ to the view of his hearers and how he used Scripture as his frame of reference in doing so. But it was not a mere informational telling about Jesus; it was a declarative report about how those hearers were themselves involved in having condemned Jesus to death—and what this meant in terms of their judgment or salvation. Peter's word to them was clear and involving; he spoke about faith, personal salvation, and the social demands that resulted from following Jesus. Knowing that his hearers were caught up in that generation's unbelief, selfishness, and the pull of its false patterns of life, Peter challenged them all, "Save yourselves from this corrupt generation" (Act 2:40b). And they accepted that challenge! What a passage for those who preach as if acting in faith is but a private affair, as if a decision to follow Christ is not also a social fact with social results to follow!

But that sermon Peter preached on the day of Pentecost shows us something more: It shows his sense of partnership as a preacher with God. Like his Lord, Peter also depended on the active presence and work of the Spirit of God while speaking his word of witness. William Barclay rightly reminded us that "the criterion by which the early Church judged a man was his relationship to the Holy Spirit. The only leaders who could lead for Christ were men who were men of the Spirit. It is even said of Jesus himself that God anointed Him with the Holy Spirit and with power (Acts 10:38)."[22] Thus our Lord's eventful preaching, and the subsequent readiness and relevance of Peter and his other event-making apostles as "they went out and proclaimed the good news everywhere, while the Lord worked with them and confirmed the message by the signs that accompanied it" (Mark 16:20 NRSV).

That is our heritage as preachers! The examples from history open new horizons for our hope. Such accounts remind us of what preaching was *then* and what it can and should be *now*— eventful! Preaching was originally meant to *do* something, to effect a difference in and for people.

In one of his books about preaching, William E. Sangster told the story about a certain seminarian who had preached before his classmates in the homiletics class. It was something of an omen if, after giving the sermon, a student was summoned to the professor's office and told to bring the sermon manuscript along. The summons had come to that student. As he entered the professor's office, the young theologian placed his manuscript on the professor's desk and sat down in silent horror, waiting as his written work was being scrutinized. The professor sat in silence too, giving the pages serious attention. His gestures of displeasure finally made the student speak up with a plea, "It will do, sir, won't it? It will do?" To which the professor gave this stinging reply: "Do what?"[23]

Our pulpit experiences will occur in many places and locales. Some preachers will preach in stately sanctuaries, some in plainly built country buildings; still others will give their witness in town halls, local school auditoriums, converted storefront buildings, or in the living room or basement of someone's home. Some might gain access to radio or television for their preaching.

---

22. William Barclay, *The Promise of the Spirit* (London: Epworth Press, 1960), 55-56.

23. William E. Sangster, *The Craft of Sermon Illustration* (Philadelphia: Westminster Press, 1950), 24-25.

But whether one's pulpit be permanent or portable, whether it be regular or improvised, part of a traditional setting or an attempt at a breakthrough in some new and previously unevangelized place, let us set ourselves to be eventful preachers whose preaching is planned and done to do something—and be a means for making a difference!

CHAPTER FIVE

The Face of Jesus:
A Sermon

For God, who said, "Let light shine out of darkness," made his light shine in our hearts to give us the light of the knowledge of the glory of God in the face of Christ. *(2 Corinthians 4:6)*

I

Paul of Tarsus was unalterably convinced that Jesus of Nazareth conspicuously reveals God to us. Paul widely and steadily sought to inform and convince others of this, sometimes reporting how he had come to this belief. In 2 Corinthians 4:6 is an allusive instance. Paul has reflected about how a redeeming glory seen in the resurrected Jesus had captured him, bequeathing a richer knowledge of God and a deeper experience than he had found as a student of Torah and life as a rabbi.

Paul had known the tradition about Moses, the revered leader whose shining face was evidence of his close walk with God, that special time with God on the mount having marked him as a special man among the people. Paul knew the report about how that splendor gave people such a shock that Moses wore a veil to shield it. Paul knew as well that the veil hid the sad fact that the splendor was steadily fading away. But now, in this text, Paul rejoiced over the undimmed, unfading glory in the face of Jesus, that glory by which he, a radically wrong religionist, had been radically illumined and spiritually redirected while traveling the road to Damascus, intent on deadly business against the church there. For Paul, the face of Jesus had been revealing, decisive, and determinative. This text is an autobiographical extract from Paul's experience. It prods and helps us to rehearse the significance of Jesus for our faith and lives. Its wording and import beckon a review of some features and fundamentals about our Lord.

II

I begin with this historical detail: *The face of Jesus was a Semitic face.*

Jesus of Nazareth was a Hebrew, part of the family line of Shem, a son of Noah. As a Semite, as that family line is described, it is likely that Jesus' physical appearance bore at least some of the features historically associated with Semitic peoples. Any proper theology about Jesus must include historical facts about him, and there is nothing more obvious in the given record than the fact that Jesus was a Hebrew, a Semite, with a face that reflected that lineage.

Next, a circumstantial detail: *The face of Jesus was the face of a sufferer.*

Jesus was born to poor parents with all that this tends to imply. Full information about the circumstances of the family is scanty, but from Luke's carefully researched report, when Jesus' mother went to offer her required religious sacrifice after his birth, her offering was "a pair of doves or two young pigeons" (Luke 2:24). This was a legal accommodation for the poor.

Growing up poor and underprivileged, growing up slighted by the privileged wealthy, growing up viewed with disdain by influential religious traditionalists, and additionally burdened as part of a minority in a homeland tyrannized by foreign Roman rule—all this caused Jesus to know torments that affect the human face, torments that usually etch lines into the human face—lines of concern over pressing needs, lines of longing for desired change, lines from sorrow and suffering.

I find myself drawn to depictions of Jesus. I have rarely seen an artist's depiction of the face of Jesus as a sufferer. Perhaps influenced more by the meaning of his life, artists may find the notion of a physically attractive Christ far more appealing—and so have theologians. But there have been some who have imaged his suffering, like Justin Martyr, whose reflections on Isaiah 53:2-3 influenced him to view those verses as a prophetic reference to Jesus as personally frail in body, small in stature, and deprived of countenance. Remembering the facts about Jesus' severely pressured life, Clement of Alexandria, Origen, and a few others thought the same.[1] It would be folly for me to be dogmatic about this, insisting on it, because no contemporary descriptions of Jesus have come down to us; we have only the record of his poverty, his struggles, his situated experiences among the disinherited, and these strongly suggest to me that the face of Jesus reflected his lot in life as a sufferer.

And now, a personality detail: *Jesus had a set face.* There is an enlightening mention in Luke's Gospel about this: "When the days drew near for him to be taken up, he set his face to go to Jerusalem" (9:51 NRSV). That expression, "set his face," is Semitic; it is a way of saying that Jesus firmed up his intention, strengthened his will, bolstered his determination to go and do that for which he had been sent.

Jesus lived intentionally. This was characteristic of him. He set himself on the side of the will of God, with strict intent to live out the insights of God's Word within him. He set himself to be with people, to be open to them, to live with concern for

---

1. See Charles Guignebert, *Jesus,* trans. Sidney H. Hook (New Hyde Park, N.Y.: University Books, Inc., 1956), 164-69.

them, and to risk himself in the interest of helping them. Personal imperative was as much a feature of his life as was integrity. This had to be so from the start, from the time he deliberated in the wilderness, weighing the issues of how he would serve the people, right through to the time he struggled so valiantly in accepting the inevitability of a cross in his future. He had to set himself *against* some things, even as he set himself *for* some others. This was crucial to Jesus, who knew himself to be on mission for God.

Thus this central theological truth about the face of Jesus: *His is the face of the Savior.* That is why Paul, in this apostolic witness, hails him as the "Christ." By "the face of Jesus Christ" Paul is referring to Jesus as the Saving Person.

III

One of the centralities of Christian faith is the teaching that Jesus came to help us to apprehend God historically, so that our personal histories can be apprehended redemptively. The first disciples of Jesus did not realize the multi-dimensional character of the life and work of Jesus until quite late, after his ascension. But once they understood his true purpose they witnessed boldly to what they had discovered about him. Interestingly, their faces became illumined by the glory they experienced through being agents of his Spirit. Jesus was at last understood as Savior and Lord, who did not belong to them alone but to everyone—his role as Savior was a universal one.

My boyhood home city of Detroit was shocked into a deepened religious awareness of this fact in 1967, in connection with something that happened to a statue of Jesus. Standing on the well-manicured lawn of Sacred Heart Seminary, just across the street from our church building, was a gray stone statue of Jesus, whose face, hands, and feet turned up black during the infamous riot that year. Those portions of that statue had not blackened from smoke from any burning buildings nearby or from any fire bomb tossed in anger against it. According to my father-in-law, who was driving along the street and saw the vandals in action, two young black boys from the community painted those parts of the statue black. From the pulpit of his church, just a few blocks further down the same street, Albert Cleage, Jr., had been preaching about Jesus as "black Messiah." Had those two boys acted to concretize that message? In pockets across the nation at about the same time, voluble voices were urging that blacks increase their militancy with the cry of "Black Power." Had those two boys caught new spirit from that slogan?

I waited to see what the white Roman Catholic officials at Sacred Heart Seminary would do. Wisely, the officials decided to leave the statue black. They thus affirmed the new coloring as a witness that Jesus is related to all, that he is the inclusive Christ who must always be understood beyond color and race considerations.

The true Christ is for all. Perhaps that repainting by those boys was an act of self-affirmation and racial pride. But it was soon understood as more: It was also an act of insight regarding the identification of Jesus with people in their situated lives. Painting black the face, hands, and feet on that gray stone statue provided occasion for a new hearing in a racially troubled city of the central biblical truth: "God was reconciling the *world* to himself in Christ" (2 Cor. 5:19, italics added).

IV

The face of Jesus is the face of the Christ who saves. It is the face of the One who has loved us all enough to catch all of us up into his own life and meaning as the Son of God.

The face of Jesus is the face of the Savior. It is his experienced, understanding face that accompanies us in our life and comforts us in our pain. It is his unselfish face that confronts us in our pride. It is his set face that calls us from our polarization and rebukes our tribal selfishness. It is his holy face that disarms and defeats the syncretistic notions urged upon us by the attempts of many to relativize the New Testament message regarding who he is.

The face of Jesus is the face of the Lord. His is the prophetic face that beckons us beyond our shortsightedness and approvingly smiles upon us when we unselfishly affirm each other, lovingly serve other people in their need, and courageously resist evil in its recognizable forms. His is the face that mercifully welcomes us when we rightly worship and honestly pray. And his is the face we will see eagerly receiving us when, at the last, Father Time will take us from Mother Earth, sending us on beyond our tasks, our times, and this troublesome shadowland of life to experience life at its best in his glorious presence.

I have been at the bedside of the godly as they took that last journey, and I remember well what some of them voiced as they looked ahead. I am thinking now about one of them. As I recited those soul-steadying lines at the close of Romans 8, which declare that not even death "will be able to separate us from the love of God that is in Christ Jesus our Lord" (Rom. 8:39), that tired, ailing believer seemed to halt her going long enough to report, in feeble but sufficient voice, "Yes, it is so, because I *see* him here with me now." That blessed believer died, basking in the glory shining upon her from the face of her Savior and Lord!

As I remember my own times of toil and strain, my own experiences of sorrow and longing, I understand the heart cry and witness of that twelfth-century pilgrim who wrote:

> Jesus, the very thought of thee
> With sweetness fills the breast;
> But sweeter far thy face to see,
> And in thy presence rest.

No voice can sing, no heart can frame,
Nor can the memory find
A sweeter sound than thy blest name,
Savior of humankind.

O hope of every contrite heart,
O joy of all the meek,
To those who fall, how kind thou art!
How good to those who seek![2]

This is also why I join with others in singing Sister Lucie
Campbell's strong statement of faith and longing:

Not just to kneel with the angels,
Nor to see loved ones who've gone,
Not just to drink at the fountain
Under the great white throne;

Not for the crown that He giveth,
That I'm trying to run this race;
all I'll want up in heaven
Is just to behold His face.

Not just to join in the chorus,
And sing with those that are blest,
And bathe my soul that is weary,
In the sea of heavenly rest,

But I'll look for the One who saved me,
From a death of sin and disgrace;
'Twill be joy when I get up in heaven,
Just to behold His face.

---

2. Translated from the Latin by Edward Caswall.

Just to behold His face,
Yes, just to behold His face;
All I will want up in heaven,
Is just to behold His face.[3]

---

3. Lucie E. Campbell, "Just to Behold His Face," 1923. See Bernice Johnson Reagon, *We'll Understand It Better By and By: Pioneering African American Gospel Composers* (Washington, D.C.: Smithsonian Institution Press, 1992), 133-34.

NAME INDEX

SCRIPTURE INDEX

251
m394

M7040-IL
2